Not My Mother's Wedding

Printed in the United States of America

ISBN: 978-0-692-00223-0
Illustrations: Guy Gilchrist
Editor: Beth Bruno

A TOAST
To Dan who Popped the Question
And
To Dad who Answered "YES!"

THANK YOU NOTES

As if planning a wedding over fourteen months wasn't enough, we had to follow it up with a year of writing about it! And like planning the wedding, our manuscript would never have taken shape without the following wonderful people. Many thanks to . . . .

Beth Bruno, our editor, for her guidance, encouragement, patience, and most of all, honesty. We wish she had been by our side when we were planning the wedding.

Guy Gilchrist, for his talent in capturing our adventure in hilarious illustrations. We wish Guy all the best as he embarks on his musical career.

Nancy Paolino and the award winning Black Tie Band. Thank you, Nancy, for getting the party started . . . and keeping it going. You never took a break all night!

A special thank you to **Matt** and **Nicole**. It was one thing having to survive the "Year of Katie." However, Katie's brother and sister were very brave by allowing us to include them in our story. We love you both very much.

CONTENTS

Maureen Chapdelaine

*invites you to join her
in an entertaining journey full of laughter,
tears and missteps as she and her daughter,*

Katie Chapdelaine

plan her marriage to

Mr. Dan Brennan

BEGINNING THE SECOND SHE GETS ENGAGED ON

Saturday, May 7th

AND NOT STOPPING UNTIL SHE WALKS DOWN THE AISLE ON

Saturday, July 8th

THEY INVITE YOU TO JOIN THEM AS THEY SHARE
THEIR ADVENTURE OF TWO GENERATIONS COMING
TOGETHER TO PLAN A TRADITIONAL WEDDING WHILE
FACING NOT ONLY THEIR OWN PERSONALITIES,
BUT ALSO THE EXPECTATIONS AND EMOTIONS OF OTHERS.

GIGGLES AND TIPS IMMEDIATELY FOLLOWING

The Proposal

The Challenge of the 50's

It happened to me . . .

I grew up in the small town of Dalton, Massachusetts, whose only claim to fame was Crane & Company, producer of all the paper used in American currency. I was a middle child, raised Roman Catholic. I remember when you could buy a McDonald's hamburger and french-fries for only a quarter. Although a decent student, I was lucky to earn a "C" in geography, as I seldom traveled beyond Berkshire County. I graduated from an all girls Catholic College located an hour drive from my home.

I married at the age of *twenty*. I had an adventurous desire to experience life outside New England. Timing is everything, and as my husband, Paul, announced a career change that allowed us to relocate, I shared news with family and friends of my pregnancy. We packed our bags and moved to Melbourne, Florida, where I gave birth to Matthew, my parents' first grandchild. Our decision to move so far away was not a big hit with either side of the family.

Two years later, Katie was born. Southern living turned out to be too slow paced for me, and I missed family. Once again, I proposed a move back to New England and Paul accommodated my request.

We bought a comfortable home in a great family neighborhood in northern Connecticut. Somehow, during those busy years of starting a family business and remodeling our home, we found time for yet another addition. Nicole was born. Not only did she round out the family, she also gave me cause to look for a bigger home.

In my *thirties,* while balancing work and raising three children, we purchased a neglected home with a saw-tooth roof on a lot with a spectacular view. The location was one of a kind . . . the house was a tear down. We leveled our investment and built the home of our dreams around an existing foundation and three rustic stone fireplaces. The neighbors thought we were crazy.

In my *forties,* I took up running; with that came the challenge of competing in road races and marathons. For many summers I begged and bribed Paul and the kids to join me at a week long running camp in Newport, RI. During the school year I helped coach indoor and outdoor track at an inner city high school.

Then I turned *fifty.*

Answering the phone one evening, I received the news from a best friend, Mo, (the other Maureen), announcing her daughter's engagement. I guess we all knew it was coming . . . but not so soon. "Wow," I exclaimed. "I am so excited for you."

I was really thinking, *Better you than me!*

Mo and I had met years earlier when our girls were defensemen on the Shooting Stars soccer team. It was a time when family togetherness took place on the sideline of travel soccer fields, the dads had a full head of hair, and survival meant carpooling and helpful friends. Despite the passage of time and the girls heading in different directions, we remained close friends.

I love a challenge. In fact, now entering middle age, I was looking forward to having more *me* time, and was thinking ahead to my next adventure. However, I have serious guidelines for taking on a new quest. I must be certain that *either* I can **control** the particulars required to complete the task, *or* that I have a graceful **escape** route should the project go awry.

To me, planning a wedding is one activity that does not fall into the category of a desired adventure. I had heard too many stories and figured out that the words **control** and **escape** were not part of the project vocabulary. I am a pants wearing, casual dining individual, frightened by the thought of being responsible for a fussy affair.

Mo invited Paul and me and a few other couples for dinner the following evening to celebrate the engagement. I decided to bring a little gift.

The next morning found me perched on a stool, green tea in hand, browsing through shelves of "Mother of the Bride" and "Wedding Planner" books. It was an uncharted section of the bookstore for me and I was overwhelmed with the number of choices.

Each book cover was more beautiful than the next. I could not stop thinking how lucky I was that I could observe my friend going through the wedding process first. Katie, my older daughter, was my only potential candidate for an engagement announcement in the near future. She had recently taken a job in Chicago, and since her boyfriend Dan was still in CT, I felt secure in the knowledge that an engagement would not be happening anytime soon.

Paul and I had not attended many weddings. In fact, this wedding would be our first wedding invitation in years. That said, being middle-aged frequently put me in the company of mothers of brides. I heard about elaborate engagement parties. Then there were the bridal showers, bridal luncheons and, of course, the wedding weekend itself. I also listened to horror stories of parents remodeling their homes in preparation for the wedding. They were exhausted, financially and physically, by the time the wedding arrived.

Knowing that I had three adult children of marrying age and a twenty year old home that needed a touch of updating, I had already put my project management skills to use. Rule #1: Plan ahead. Update the home before the announcement of an engagement.

I had approval from my CFO (Chief Financial Officer aka Paul) to make major home improvements during the upcoming summer months. Paul agreed to my suggestion of connecting the house to the garage, giving us a much-needed back entry with closet space and an updated guest bath. Over time, the project grew into a complete remodel of the existing kitchen. I had designed and contracted Paul's last two office buildings, so he felt confident to give approval and walk away. (During such projects, Paul and I would use the same vocabulary, but I am not sure he ever realized I was a bit more liberal on some definitions. A good example is the word "budget".)

And it can happen to you . . .

I chose a wedding planning book and a funny Mother of the Bride book as gifts for Mo. Regardless of how the wedding year went down, she had to keep her sense of humor. I find that true for life in general. I finished my tea, picked up a few more kitchen design magazines and headed home to meet the builder and check out the progress on the new foundation. I was happy. I was busy. Now if I could only make a decision on the new cabinets and appliances. Let's see: cherry or off white, Wolf or Viking, gas or electric.

I pulled into the driveway to find six men wearing poker faces peering into a hole of freshly poured concrete. I parked the Jeep, let the dog out to join the workers and went directly to check for phone messages. **Big mistake.**

Line one and Line two: two new messages.

"Hi, Mrs. Chappy. It's Dan. Just calling to see if you and Mr. Chappy will be around on Saturday. I have something to ask you and was hoping we could meet for lunch. Give me a call at work, or you have my cell number if that's better. It's poker night so I'd love to talk before I leave at 8:00. Later."

Thursday 11:32 am

I want to say I went numb. I wish I had gone numb. But my stomach hurt too much. *This can't be what I think it is. No way!* The dog wants in. The doorbell is ringing.

Message two.

"Hey, Mrs. Chappy. Don't tell Kate I'm coming, OK? I want it to be a surprise."

Thursday 11:36 am

End of final message.

I opened the door, tripped over the dog, saw concern in the builder's eyes, and started to cry!

KISS

I believe in the KISS method – *Keep It Simple Stupid.* I have never had a closet filled with designer clothing and handbags. You will never open my fridge and find endless options for breakfast, lunch and dinner at your fingertips. Not that I can't afford to treat myself, or there aren't times when I wish I had more choices, but it would drive me crazy. I do not like to make decisions and by following the KISS method, I don't have to. Whether it's deciding what outfit to wear to work, what to eat for breakfast or which hair gel to use in the morning, I figure the fewer choices the better.

Therefore, I keep things simple. I have black shoes that match my black pants and gray pants, both of which will go with any no-iron, pastel, button-down shirt I decide to throw on for work. Every morning I blow-dry my hair and pull it back in a low pony-tail. Yogurt, fruit, chicken and salad are my three meals a day . . . everyday. In addition, I have two cats that look identical. Life is uncomplicated.

Thankfully, I met Dan. While Dan can handle complexity, he doesn't need much to make him happy and he is incredibly laid back. He is perfectly happy eating chicken and rice every night for dinner, and, fortunately for me, he loves yogurt. It doesn't hurt that he grew up in a household where "a place for everything and everything in its place" was a family motto. Oh, and although he owns a pair of brown shoes, I notice he only wears his black ones because it is easier. He is my kind of guy.

After growing up, graduating college and working . . . all in Connecticut . . . I was becoming restless. I have heard it said that no one ever likes their first job, and mine was no exception. I needed a change.

Chicago had become home to my brother Matt, shortly after he graduated from college in Ohio. I rallied Dan and my family's support in my desire to venture West and join him. Besides leaving Dan, another downside would be leaving my two cats, Ben and Jerry. Dan had bought Ben and Jerry for me our first year after college and they had quickly become part of our life. Dan and I never had another quiet moment alone on the couch after they came along. It was always Dan, Ben and Jerry, and me watching movies or eating dinner together. They even slept in bed with me at night. I knew I couldn't leave if it meant losing my boys. After a few tears and a little begging, Dan offered to let them move in with him.

The timing seemed to work out and my very social brother from Chicago was looking to rent out his extra bedroom. It was the perfect place for a much-needed change of scenery. I packed my bags and headed off to the Windy City. Little did I know that my brother was a little too social to have his younger sister in the room next door. Before I unpacked my bags, he sent me off to live with one of his friends down the street. It was the best decision either of us could have made.

I didn't really have any plans when I moved to Chicago. It was just a chance to do something fun. However, having fun meant having money. Thanks to my new roommate and all of her connections, within two weeks I found myself working full time at an Event Planning company in downtown Chicago and working nights at a busy restaurant. As my free time disappeared and my bank account grew, I stopped thinking about anything that did not involve work or sleep.

For five straight months, I worked long hours and spent any free time I had exploring Chicago and talking on the phone with Dan. We would update each other on what was going on in our lives, how my cats were doing and when our next visit would be. Upon seeing our phone bills, we decided to keep it a bit shorter on the phone. We just talked about how much we missed each other. We spent the money we saved purchasing plane tickets.

Dan and I had never talked about getting married – at all. I knew we were both comfortable in the relationship, and neither of us had reason to worry about the other. We were very committed to each other and that was enough at the time. We met in college during a calculus class, but didn't really start speaking to each other until one night at the end of our freshman year. We started "officially" dating at the beginning of our sophomore year when we were just 19. I don't think at the age of 24 it had hit us (or at least me) yet, that I was actually old enough to get married. Besides, my brother and Dan's sister were two years older than we were and I assumed they would get married first.

Three months after I moved to Chicago I went home to Connecticut to visit Dan for a weekend and to celebrate Mother's Day with my family. I had been working for 10 days straight. All I could think about was relaxing with Dan. I hadn't packed a single article of nice clothing because in my mind we weren't doing anything that involved leaving Dan's apartment. I had packed three pairs of elastic waistband sweatpants and a variety of my favorite armpit-stained running shirts. It was going to be fantastic.

Dan has never been one to suggest going out to eat, preferring to cook for me in the comfort of his own home. I was shocked when he insisted that we go out to dinner while I was visiting. I explained to him that I had not packed any "going out" clothes other than my "going out for a run" attire.

"Then let's go shopping," he said. "I could use a new shirt myself."

I should have suspected that something was up. Dan, who doesn't like to eat out and hates to shop, was insisting that we go out to dinner and go to a clothing store. Was this the same guy I left behind? Could someone change that much in only three short months?

I was exhausted and didn't want to argue. I figured that I would at least get treated to a nice lunch while shopping. We headed to Southport.

One black pair of pants and a new top later I was ready for dinner. Sad that I was going to have to leave Ben and Jerry, I gave them both an extra hug as we were walking out the door. Jerry, being the mama's boy that he is, made sure to rub against my leg one last time before we left. Buckling my seat belt, I panicked when I looked down at my fuzzy pants and remembered the one drawback to owning cats. HAIR! Dan grabbed my hand as I reached to open the glove compartment to get the roll of tape I kept there for just such emergencies.

"I needed the tape to wrap my mother's gift and brought it into the house. Wait here . . . I'll go get it," he told me as he rushed inside.

Upon returning, I laughed and thanked Dan for being so nice. As he turned on some classical music, he looked at me and said, "I am trying to act more like an adult."

Looking back at this moment, it blows my mind that I didn't realize what was going on.

Dan had made reservations at our favorite restaurant. The restaurant was right on the water in Westport, Connecticut. It had threatened to rain earlier that morning, but had since cleared up and turned into a beautiful day. It was such a picturesque evening as we drove along the ocean's edge and into Southport that I cringed at the thought of my original plan to spend the evening curled up on the couch.

The best part of the evening was that I was relaxed. I had missed Dan, and my visit home was turning out better than

I expected. I have to admit, quiet time with Dan in a fancy restaurant beat quiet time with Dan on his hand-me-down sofa.

As we enjoyed our meal, we discussed a friend who had told everyone he would be proposing to his girlfriend soon. I laughed and let Dan know that when he proposed to me he better make sure I had a nice manicure and my hair looked good. Again, I probably should have taken a hint when Dan looked at my nails and turned pale, but I didn't.

After a wonderful dinner, Dan suggested we go to the beach. I thought this was a great idea and asked if we should head back up the street a bit to the public beach in Southport. Dan insisted we stay in Westport. Westport has some of the most beautiful beaches, if not *the* most beautiful beaches in New England. The only drawback to visiting the Westport beaches is that they are not open to the public. (Thanks to the wealth and celebrity status of many of its residents.) I was not thrilled that we were going to have to argue with one of the many guards protecting the beach or pay him to let us enter. I was surprised when the guard let us right in. I figured he would hit us up on the way out.

The beach was quiet and as the sun started to set Dan and I walked out on a rock wall that jutted into the water. Dan looked at me and jokingly asked, "Had a manicure or a haircut lately?" I think at that point I started to laugh and then stopped breathing as Dan got down on one knee and proposed. All I could think of was how fortunate I was to be marrying my best friend. There was no doubt in my mind that my answer would be yes, and that I was the luckiest girl to have found such a wonderful man. Not only was I marrying a great guy, but I also knew my friends and family loved him just as much as I did. As Dan went to grab the camera and champagne he had hidden in the car, I thought, *How the hell did he pull this off without my parents or me finding out?*

Dan and I spent the next few hours on the beach enjoying champagne and talking about his every move for the past few weeks. For the next 16 hours I was on cloud nine.

The next day was Mother's Day and Dan and I could not wait to get to my parents' house to tell them all about the previous day. Upon arriving home, we chatted with my parents and grandmother about how Dan proposed. We popped champagne and made a toast. After dinner, my mother turned to me and asked, "Have you thought about a venue for your reception yet?"

"What?" I hadn't even thought I would be getting engaged for the next few years. How was I supposed to come up with a venue for my wedding in a 24-hour period? I could not believe it! It had not been a full day yet and already I was supposed to have made decisions! I almost spit my champagne back into the glass.

Little did I realize the year I had ahead of me was going to be one of the toughest and funniest years of my life!

The Reception Venue

The Research Project

What makes putting on a wedding so difficult is that you have to back into the planning. I have read that most couples are engaged an average of 14 months. Yet, even with this generous time frame, the Bride and Groom are rushed into picking a date and booking a reception venue before they have had time to consider the significance and implications of their decisions.

Paul and I sat on pins and needles waiting for the phone to ring. My mother was spending Mother's Day weekend with us, and my brother had joined us for dinner. They were unaware that Katie would become engaged that very evening to a guy who had stolen our hearts, or . . . . she would be crushing many hearts with one blow.

"She said yes!" I screamed, holding the phone, as Katie continued speaking. "Katie and Dan are getting married! They are driving up to see us tomorrow."

The following day was a celebration of hugs, picture taking and champagne. Katie and Dan had a glow about them. They were so happy and in love. You could see it and feel it.

As the afternoon was winding down, I suddenly realized that Katie would be heading back to Chicago the next morning. I had made a mental note that to discuss wedding planning on this day would be inappropriate, ill timed and unappreciated. With time ticking away, I found myself getting antsy. My Type A personality was kicking in, as was reality. I flitted around. I moved knick-knacks. I fussed over the dog. My insides felt like an erupting volcano.

I sat down to join the group gathered in the front room as they reminisced about Katie and Dan's first date, and before my back end hit the chair my mouth was open and I blurted, "So, guys, have you thought at all about where you would like to hold your reception?"

"We talked about that on the ride home," said Katie. "We were thinking of being married by the water."

Water . . . what water?

"Oh, wow." *Think, Maureen . . . think.* "Oh, wow . . . ."

I sat on my hands. *Come on, Paul, say something! Does the dog need to be walked? Please . . . don't let me talk.*

"Gee, I always thought you would get married in town," I said, trying to be nonchalant. "I never thought of a destination wedding."

"A destination wedding? Who said anything about an island?" Katie asked.

Silence . . . . . .

"I'd love more coffee," Grandma said, handing me her half-full cup.

My stomach flipped as Katie and Dan's car drove out of sight. It was not a case of the Sunday night blues. It was worse. I realized that I was facing a huge undertaking for which I had no experience, no networking group and no escape route. Within minutes, I had alienated my co-worker for this project even before the planning had begun.

I knew in my heart that Katie and Dan deserved time to enjoy the newness of their engagement. Even I did not want to be cheated out of enjoying this wonderful time in my daughter's life.

Nevertheless, I was now a month into watching Mo try to choose a reception site for her daughter. Her feedback was not encouraging. "These places are booked so far in advance," she moaned. "Saturday nights are almost non-existent."

So much for basking in the moment.

I was also concerned about the cost of a wedding. From the start, Paul had a number in mind and felt confident that his estimation was what a wedding *would* cost. I have never asked him where he got that figure; I was certain he would not have an answer. I do believe that what he meant to say was, "I am confident in my estimation of what a wedding *should* cost." He appeared quite comfortable with his calculation. I practiced the philosophy, *If it works, don't fix it.* I figured it was too early to discuss the budget anyway.

Years earlier, I had been assigned the task of locating office space to accommodate the growing family business. I began by asking questions. "How many employees will work at the facility? What are the location requirements? How will the space be used? What's my budget?"

Now, given the assignment to locate a wedding site by the water on a Saturday night the following summer was tough enough. Not knowing how many guests would be invited, if people would be willing to travel, and the cost of the many vendors for budgeting purposes made it a crapshoot.

I finally realized that sitting at home was not getting the job done. Now my turn, I entered the bookstore with confidence and determination, headed directly to the Wedding section (without asking for directions) and purchased my very own *Ultimate Wedding Planner.*

Back home I searched the Internet and printed out information on every wedding venue along the Connecticut shoreline. I discovered that each location offered the Bride a unique wedding experience, some formal and some casual. I began to realize that *by the water* was only one line item on a list of possible requirements for the wedding Katie and Dan had in mind. It was time for on-site visits.

Days later, my youngest daughter, Nicole, arrived home from college for summer vacation. I swung the front door open, held her tight, took a big deep breath and said, "I'm so happy to have you home! Do you want to go sightseeing?"

Anywhere But Here

Immediately following our engagement, I was still living in Chicago and Dan was living in Connecticut. We weren't exactly a hop, skip, and a jump away from each other. It was not easy for us to find the time to be together and make on-site visits to wedding venues. So we asked my mother to accept the mission – find the location for our reception!

Dan and I are not Type A personalities; in fact, some people might argue that we are too laid back. My mother, on the other hand, is a freight train when she wants to get things done. This created a bit of tension when it came to finding a location for our wedding reception. While Dan and I wanted a place where our guests could come, enjoy a nice meal, dance, and preferably have a water view, my mother did not care so much where we had the wedding, as long as it was nice, and we could book it NOW.

Despite the fact that my mom did not want to have a *destination wedding,* she caved and allowed us to look an hour south of my hometown at venues that were along the Connecticut shoreline. The first place we visited was beautiful. It was on the water, had scenic ocean views and was not too far from home. The only problem was it could host three weddings on the same day. Now I love my friends and my family, but we do tend to get a bit unruly when we party. I had visions of my brother making out with the bride in the next room while my sister puked on the groom being married down the hall. My concerns, based on weekends of partying with my siblings, did not dissuade my mother. The wedding venue had availability for the following summer and she lobbied to book it!

After a little coaxing and support from my sister, my mother agreed to look at other locations. The next reception venue we visited had a calming view of a lake, hosted only one wedding at a time, and was within an hour's drive of our home. This, according to my mom, kept it from being a *destination wedding*. Again, there was a problem. The venue, an early 20th century French Tudor estate, must have belonged to a pack rat at one point who had an affinity for portraits of old people. The walls of the reception hall were covered in faces. Scary faces. Sad faces. Dead faces. No matter where you walked you always felt like someone was watching you. For the bride who could not bear to have a shower because people would have to watch her opening gifts, this was going to be too much!

I tried to stop the freight train with gentle suggestions that people might not feel comfortable having dead faces stare at them while they tried to eat dinner. This did not work. That is when my sister stepped in and stood on the tracks until the train at least slowed down. My sister, Nicole, is not rude or mean, but demanding and persistent have been used to describe her. She also felt this was just as much her wedding as it was mine. She did not like the inside of this venue and let my mother know it. It was moldy and old. It was not what she envisioned for her sister's wedding. Not only did she not like the inside, but the dreary outside did not suit her either. She stood her ground long enough to divert the freight train in another direction.

Despite the fact that our options were dwindling, I had one firm requirement for my venue other than the ocean view. I did not want it to have a carpet. No matter how hard people try, I always find that carpeted banquet halls and hotels give off that "convention center feeling." I will blame this hang-up on my time spent in Event Planning. No matter how many flowers the bride puts in the room, or how high she upgrades her linens, the carpet usually does not match the bridal theme and the room screams *banquet hall.* I believe it is what my mother is referring to when she says, "Trying to put pearls on a pig." No matter what you do to try and make the venue look as if it was built for a wedding, you just aren't going to be able to cover up that *one size fits all* impression. Unfortunately, the requirement of hardwood floors throughout the venue was limiting our choices in Connecticut even more.

Out of desperation, my parents suggested that we go to Newport, Rhode Island to look at a few locations they felt might work. While there, we stumbled upon the perfect setting for our wedding, complete with a large lawn, privacy from the public, ocean views and breathtaking gardens. The inside was just as spectacular. The expansive ballroom with its beautifully maintained hardwood floors and gilded mirrors that reflected the sparkling ocean views was amazing. Even the bathrooms had an air of elegance. Better yet, there were a few dates available that we felt would work. We had found our venue!

While it scares me to think I could have been married in the house of horrors with faces watching my every move, it scares me more to think that I could still be engaged and looking for the perfect venue. In the end, my mother's persistence found us the perfect wedding site on a perfect summer day in July. If I had to do it again I would not let her energized personality frighten me as much as it did. I would have found a good seat on the non-stop train and let her do her thing until she found something that worked for all of us.

The Church

Accepting Donations

When the Catholic Church began making headline news in the mid '90s for reported indiscretions with young children, I decided I had enough. Being raised as a Catholic, I had struggled with being held to a higher standard, and carrying the weight of guilt when I failed. As an adult, I decided the time had come to take a break and rethink my stand on religious institutions.

My religious rebellion was perfectly timed. The kids had completed religious education and received the required Church sacraments of First Communion and Confirmation. Living on their own, they were now responsible for their own souls. I do not recall a discussion or debate on the topic, but Paul and I simply stopped attending Mass.

Of course, not belonging to a parish is a real *gotcha*. During my religious hiatus, I was uncomfortable knowing that should we need the services of a church, we would be out of luck. As the years passed, I acknowledged that should it be a wedding or a ritual of some other kind, being affiliated with a parish has its benefits. Long before the hint of a wedding, I made an appointment at the rectory, registered as a parish member, and left carrying my donation envelopes.

As it turned out, my forward thinking and weekly contributions were unnecessary on two accounts.

Obvious is the fact that Katie and Dan chose to be married out of town.

Not obvious was that Katie was no longer considered a parish member anyway. She was an adult, living on her own, and presumably a member of her *own* parish. Even choosing to marry in town would require her to apply, and pay, as a non-parishioner.

I sulked for an entire morning over my mistaken logic about needing to become a parish member. Nevertheless, I now needed to find a church in Rhode Island to perform the wedding ceremony. I discovered that parishes, regardless of religion, are not always willing to marry non-parishioners. I made many inquiries into parish policies, which frequently resulted in a sermon on the mount before the words, "I am sorry, we cannot help you," were spoken.

I do believe in God, and, yes, I would like to see my children married in a religious ceremony. Yet, while struggling to find a parish that 1) performed wedding ceremonies for non-parishioners and 2) had availability on the two dates available at our venue, I suggested we change religious affiliation if only for that weekend. I prayed for a miracle!

After going through this process, I can understand why parishes are not so open to serving non-members and I do not blame them. The necessary phone calling, paper processing and coordination to execute a wedding ceremony is enormous. That said, for the right amount of money, anything is possible, and there are those parishes, thank the Lord, that are willing to provide the service.

The Internet is a wonderful tool and I finally identified two Catholic Churches in the area that would marry Katie and Dan. I called each parish to obtain their specific requirements, available dates, and the time of day open for wedding ceremonies. I then contacted our wedding venue and inquired about their experiences with these churches.

The first parish had a reputation for working easily with the bride and groom. The pastor performed the service himself and allowed the couple to personalize their ceremony. The church had a contemporary architectural flair and was located less than 15 minutes from the reception venue.

The second parish, although closer to the reception site, had a more traditional facade, strict rules and rigid requirements. An elderly nun was responsible for the coordination of all weddings held in the parish. She was known for performing her job with dedicated detail. Sister validated her reputation after only one brief phone conversation. Having attended 12 years of parochial school, and having my bottom whacked for using incorrect math procedures at the blackboard in third grade, **I** voted for the angular-shaped church.

"I am not getting married in a church that looks like it has sunk into the ground and all that is left is the roof," exclaimed Katie. "I refuse to get married in a pyramid." It was obvious that Katie was not going to choose a contemporary building when the alternative was being married in a beautiful stone church with large stained-glass windows.

Katie sensed my hesitation. She knew the nun in charge, a Bride of Christ, scared me. "Listen, Dan has asked to be involved in planning the wedding. What if we book the church and ask Dan to be Sister's contact person? I know he won't mind."

"Right," I said. "This is exactly how Mother-in-Laws get a bad reputation. One call to Sister and he'll hate me for life!"

Things have a way of working out. We booked the traditional looking church after intense praying and a sizeable financial *donation*. Katie and Dan also paid with a donation of Sunday afternoons attending premarital religious education classes. I always told Katie there would be paybacks for the lectures I had to endure from her CCD teachers. And Dan? He and Sister hit it off just fine. The paperwork was processed and my reputation as a Mother-in-Law was saved. Miraculously, my prayers were answered.

The Bad Habit

I had grown up hearing my parents' stories about attending Catholic school as children and I always found them fascinating. My father told us that the nuns did not really have feet, but that they rolled around on skates under their habits. My mother talked about sneaking off to see the boys on other campuses while attending an all girls Catholic College. It all sounded like so much fun. There was never any talk of being hit with rulers or sent to the confessional when we reminisced over their Catholic School days at the dinner table.

My family was not overly religious, but while we were young my siblings and I were herded to church every Sunday for Mass, which was immediately followed by CCD (Sunday school). We all made it through First Communion, but as travel soccer and hockey games started to take over the Sunday morning slot, my parents decided that it was okay to go to Sunday Mass on Saturday evenings. As we all got older and headed off to college, Saturday Mass slowly became Christmas and Easter only.

Dan's family had experienced a similar decline in attending Mass, as I'm sure many busy families do over time. Despite this dwindling commitment to attending church, Dan and I still wanted to get married in a Catholic ceremony. We felt with the current divorce rate, having God on our side couldn't hurt. Again, we had recruited my mom to help us locate a church that would marry us. My grandparents had been strict Catholics and my mom had grown up in a house where church always came first. We felt with her background she would be the best person to handle this task.

With this new job in hand, the freight train got right on track and started her search of Catholic churches in the Newport area. It didn't take her long to come up with a list of churches and for Dan and me to be turned down by most of them, as we were not members of the parish. Finally we chose a church that would marry us. The next step was to meet the nun in charge.

You can imagine my surprise at what happened the weekend my mom and I went to visit the church where Dan and I would be getting married. We had just arrived in Newport, and we were not going to meet Sister until the next morning. My mom wanted a look at the inside of the church so we decided to stop by to see if the doors were open. As we pulled into the parking lot, there was a skeletal old woman dressed in a habit about to enter the church. I looked at my mom and said, "That must be Sister." Before the words escaped my mouth, I felt the car fly forward. In shock, I looked over at my mother to see what had happened and to my horror found her head below the steering wheel as she pressed on the gas and flew down the street to safety.

As soon as we were back on the main road I asked my mom what was wrong. She pulled herself together and calmly explained that her lovely pink sweater set and white Capri pants were not appropriate attire for meeting a nun. I was suspicious of this explanation.

It was not until the next day while sitting in the vestibule with Sister that I realized what an effect the Catholic Church had on my mother. I would not say my mother is a stubborn person, but she is quick to stand her ground in any situation . . . and will get to her desired result any way she can. Trying to win Sister over, she jokingly asked, "Would it be alright if we had the vocalist sing 'Oh Danny Boy' during the service?" I watched in terror as Sister scolded my mother for asking her to play such an ethnic song in the Catholic Church during a wedding ceremony of all occasions! Mom turned a funny shade of red and sank further down in her seat. Upon leaving, I found my mother looking a few inches shorter and suffering from dry mouth.

Safe in the car, my mother blurted, "You mentioned that Dan asked to help out with the wedding planning. I'll risk my reputation as the perfect mother-in-law. Going forward, Dan will be Sister's contact. There is no hazard pay."

Although I saw the inside of the church for all of five minutes, I left with a good feeling. I never thought to ask if the church was air-conditioned (it was not), or if the organist was included in the price of admission (he was not). It didn't matter. Almost every other area church had turned us down, as we were not part of the parish. God's House apparently turned into a member's only club when couples were from out of town.

Despite my mother's childhood "issues," Sister was our last chance. While she was tough on us the year we spent meeting with her to plan the ceremony, she had a job to do. By the time the rehearsal rolled around she even felt comfortable joking with us. In the end Sister turned out to be a Godsend instead of another bad habit.

The Engagement Party

No Gifts Please

I recently figured out why my successfully employed son is still thrilled to receive a 50-dollar bill with his occasional note from Grandma. He is broke from attending so many weddings! That is exactly why, when planning Katie and Dan's Engagement Party, I suggested printing No Gifts Please on the invitations.

Keep in mind I was still in shock from planning a *destination wedding,* during peak season, in a popular resort location. I had concern for the money friends and family would have to spend to attend the event. My family is small but very close. I had no doubt they would want to be present at the wedding. However, I did not want to risk hard feelings over the cost they would incur in travel and lodging for their families. Our list of invited friends was also small, and it was important to me that we not create a situation preventing them from joining our family in the celebration.

A neighbor's son was a groomsman in a recent wedding. "They kept it simple," she chuckled, referring to the bride and groom. "They held a small informal wedding on Block Island. That kept the cost down for their families, but the bridal party incurred the cost of flying to New England, taking a ferry to Block Island, and paying the price for an in-season hotel. Add the wedding attire and gift, and the total goes even higher."

Back in the day, weddings were more compact. Attending a wedding rarely required booking airfare. Rehearsal dinners were not pre-wedding receptions, and if my friends were having engagement parties, I was not invited.

"I'm not choosing sides on this issue, babe, but what do those Wedding Planner books I find all over the house recommend?" Paul asked after one of my soul-searching monologues on the topic of gift giving.

It seems even the professionals can't decide.

"Well, in Emily Post's book called **Etiquette,** she says, 'Traditionally gifts for the couple are not brought to the engagement party.'"

Then, **The Everything Wedding Etiquette Book** tells me, "Gifts aren't required, but just in case, you may want to begin by spreading word of where you've registered."

"That was helpful," Paul sighed, relieved that it was trash night and happy to have an escape.

What I was not thinking at the time, or did not realize, was that *destination wedding* or not, to attend a wedding today requires travel by most guests. The groom's family ends up traveling regardless, unless fortunate to be from the bride's location. High school classmates left town years ago. College friends entering the working world are scattered everywhere. Even immediate families no longer live in close proximity.

When *we* left college, the tendency was to keep in touch with your roommate and perhaps one or two best friends. Today, with e-mail and texting being relatively inexpensive, it becomes possible to maintain friendships with many classmates regardless of where they live. I envy my kids for having so many close friends. Although they live a distance apart, they stay in each other's lives and visit as time permits.

The ability to stay connected with friends has an impact on the bottom line of a wedding guest list. I listen to the *20-* and *30-somethings* say they are on the *wedding circuit.* Many weekends they travel to attend the weddings of friends from high school and college, along with the occasional cousin and work associate.

Does it hit their wallets? You bet. Would they miss a wedding? Not if they can help it.

"When I invited my entire fourth grade class to the skating rink for my birthday party and you wrote NO GIFTS PLEASE on the invitation, I wasn't paying attention," Katie recalled. "Printing NO GIFTS PLEASE on my Engagement Party invitations – **TACKY!**"

I lost focus on the rationale for gift giving. Perhaps not all, but many young couples sleep on futons and cook with microwaves. The bestowing of gifts on an engaged couple helps them get started in their roles as husband and wife. Just as Katie and Dan were receiving gifts, they will be expected to give gifts in the future.

Times have changed, and again, I woke up to a new reality. Even if Katie had married locally, only a small number of guests would be spared the cost of travel. Katie and I still debate the definition of a *destination wedding*. Nevertheless, the fact remains that Katie and Dan's wedding was conventional. Once again, I found myself playing *mother* to the rest of the world, at the expense of my own daughter.

I may plan a House Warming party to celebrate the purchase of Katie and Dan's first home. If you are invited, don't look for the suggestion of NO GIFTS PLEASE on the invitation.

To Gift . . . Or Not to Gift

I've never thought it was fair that a bride should suffer through a bridal shower while her fiancé plays golf. When my mom suggested throwing an engagement party, I thought it was a wonderful way to avoid the embarrassment of opening gifts in front of a room full of *soon to be family* but *currently complete strangers*. I also liked knowing that Dan would be there with me, so I didn't have to go it alone. It was the perfect combination of getting to know the new extended family without the formality of opening gifts.

We were excited to see friends we hadn't seen since our engagement and I was looking forward to a good time. While putting together the guest list you can imagine my shock when my mom suggested putting *No Gifts Please* on the invitations. Wouldn't it be presumptuous to assume people felt they needed to bring gifts? Moreover, putting *No Gifts Please* on the invitation is the equivalent of your mom looking at your dad and saying, "Oh no, honey, I don't mind doing the dishes." You know she really wants the help. I felt it was a signal to our guests that while we didn't expect gifts, they would be welcome.

My mom had been reading every bridal book on the market. Due to the mixed signals on gift giving in these books, my mom felt it would be best to communicate our stance on gift giving. I had not read these books. When I receive an invitation to a shower or wedding, it usually includes details about where the bride and groom have registered for gifts. Engaged couples create Web sites so guests know exactly what kind of china they would like for their wedding. Dan and I hadn't even thought about registering before our engagement party. The fact that this information was not splashed at the bottom of the invitation or posted online should have been a big enough hint that we were NOT looking for gifts.

When I mentioned this to my mother, she threw back her second argument in what was quickly becoming a heated debate. She explained that weddings cost too much for the guests and that she did not want them to feel they needed to spend more money for this party. I agreed with her. In the course of the year you have to pay for travel, hotel rooms, shower gifts, and wedding gifts. By the time the wedding comes along it's possible to have spent hundreds of dollars on a couple. I just couldn't wrap my head around the idea that people actually thought they should bring a gift to an engagement party.

Therefore, I vetoed the idea of *No Gifts Please* on the invitation.

I was amazed at what happened at the engagement party. People actually brought gifts! Apparently, my mother wasn't the only one reading the books that said you should bring a gift to an engagement party. Whoops. Looking back, it would have made sense to tell guests that this was a time to celebrate the engagement. We wanted friends and family from both sides to get together – giving them a chance to meet each other prior to the wedding. I wish I could say I always agreed when my mother dove into her bridal books and told me what was best from that moment on . . . but I didn't. At times, I was right and everything worked out, but most of the time, I regretted not listening to her advice (or the advice the book had given her). It wasn't my last "whoops" moment that year.

The Budget

Only Answer the Question

From the moment an engagement is announced, the banter surrounding the cost of the impending wedding is as commonplace as the gestures of celebration.

I always assumed, but we never discussed, that when the girls got married Paul and I would pay for their weddings. There was never any reason for Katie to think otherwise.

Happy for Katie and Dan, and now playing his new role as Father of the Bride, Paul began his lament of *what this wedding is going to cost me* with good humor and a sense of pride. Where he came up with his estimated budget, however, I will never know. It was off the charts . . . and aimed in the wrong direction.

Perhaps that is why, when wedding plans got underway, Katie came to *me* with the question, "Mom, have you and Dad talked about a budget?"

I suppose, like Paul, I could have tossed out a number I thought to be both reasonable and affordable. But without the details to support that number, I knew the budget would be meaningless. As with locating a reception venue, I found myself *backing into* a budget, rather than *planning with* a budget.

It is only in hindsight I came to discover that the terms *Wedding Budget* and *Average Wedding Cost* are over-used and under-defined.

Wedding Budget

There is no reliable definition for the term *Wedding Budget*. Conventionally, the *Wedding Budget* includes costs associated with the wedding *ceremony* and wedding *reception*. In reality, wedding expenses begin at the time of engagement and can accumulate until days after the bride walks down the aisle.

Would it be fair to exclude any of the following from the cost of putting on a wedding, regardless of who is paying for them?

Potential Wedding Year Expenses

- Family dinner to congratulate the recently engaged couple.
- Dinner out to meet and welcome the groom's family.
- Printing and mailing of Save the Date notices.
- Printing and mailing of Engagement Party Invitations.
- Repairs to the home for purposes of hosting the Engagement party/and or the Wedding weekend.
- Cost of Engagement Party.
- Expenses incurred during weekends home by the bride and groom for purposes of wedding planning.
- Repairs to mother of the bride for purposes of looking her best at the wedding. (Reference: *Just The Way You Are*)
- Trial hair and makeup consultation for the Bride and Mother of the Bride.
- Bridal shower expenses for mother and siblings: travel, gift giving and/or hosting the event.
- Wedding Consultant.
- Planning trips for purposes of booking hotels, researching florists, musicians and tastings at preferred caterers.

- Travel and meal expenses incurred while in search of bridal and bridesmaid attire.
- Travel expenses incurred flying/transporting siblings home for wedding related events.
- Wedding trousseau for bride: engagement party attire, shower attire, honeymoon outfits.
- Mother of the Bride attire and accessories, lunches with friends to discuss appropriateness of said attire, travel expenses for fittings.
- Cost of Father of the Bride attire, and dinner out while reserving said attire.
- Cost of wedding attire for Bride's siblings and possibly grandparents.
- Cost of housing extended family during wedding weekend.
- Cost of housing bridal party during wedding weekend.
- Cost of entertaining during wedding weekend.
- Bridal luncheon hosted by Bride.
- Printing and postage for Thank You notes.
- Professional cleaning and acid-free, Museum Style Storage of the Bridal Gown.

Then there is the cost of the **Rehearsal Dinner** and **Honeymoon.**

Average Wedding Cost

Average Wedding Cost is defined by statistics gathered nationwide and can vary greatly based on where you live, and more importantly, what type of wedding you have in mind. In addition, *Average Wedding Cost* (like *Wedding Budget*) is usually calculated on a number representing the wedding day itself and is not all inclusive of monies spent during the planning period. Until the government sees the need to define what should be included in the cost of an average wedding for tax purposes, I suspect the definition will continue to be less than complete.

According to the National Association of Wedding Ministers Wedding Statistics:

- Currently, the average amount spent on a traditional American wedding is around $30,000.

- Las Vegas, Nevada is the most popular wedding destination in the country, reporting 100,000 weddings a year. (Chapels in Las Vegas advertise wedding ceremonies beginning as low as $149.00. I wonder if these figures are included in the average cost of a U.S. wedding.)

- Twenty-eight percent of weddings taking place in the U.S. serve only cake and punch at the reception. (That figure will influence the bottom line for Average Cost and be misleading to those planning a buffet or sit-down dinner.)

So when Dad rolls his eyes, as Fathers of the Bride do, and quotes the *Average Cost* of a wedding breaking the bank, it is best to gently console him and cautiously change the subject.

How was I to foresee in advance the depth and breadth of expenses that are part of planning a traditional wedding? How was I to answer Paul when he would ask, "So, honey, are we still on budget?"

Fortunately for me there was one project management technique I **was** able to apply to wedding planning. NEVER LIE . . . BUT ONLY ANSWER THE QUESTION.

> *"Katie's gown is beautiful. How much?"*
> Answer: $$$$ (Cost of veil, tiara, broach for dress, undergarments not included.)

> *"Does the band play during cocktail hour?"*
> Answer: Yes (At an additional charge.)

"We have to serve Tanguery & Jack Daniels."
Answer: No problem. (That is called an upgrade.)

"How many limousines will we need?"
Answer: Two (And one very large party bus.)

"Are you paying for all the bridesmaids to get their hair and makeup done?"
Answer: No, dear. (Just their hair.)

"Are we having a breakfast for the guests the morning after the wedding?"
Answer: No, dear. (Not at this moment, but only because I have not planned it yet.)

"Is the Bridal Shower this weekend? Was Katie able to book a hotel room for you and Nicole in Boston at a reasonable rate?"
Answer: Yes, dear. (Considering the only room left in the city was a suite at the Omni Parker complete with in-room exercise equipment, I would say it was a decent price.)

"I have to tell you, I love your dress."
Answer: Thanks! (What you are really going to love is the special order jewelry I have purchased to complement the outfit.)

I can now empathize with the Father of the Bride who says with a shrug, "I just opened my wallet."

Coco Chanel Said It Best

Dan and I were never given a budget for our wedding. However, when my mom told me the Passat was the only **VW** I would ever own, I knew I wouldn't be wearing a **V**era **W**ang gown on my wedding day. Dan and I would have to set boundaries when it came to wedding spending. My parents would respect us for following their example of not being excessive.

Although my father owns a successful business, he does not lead a lifestyle of overindulgence. In his down time, he enjoys the simple pleasures of sleeping in front of the TV and gardening. While these could be inexpensive activities, the way in which he accomplishes them is anything but. When he sleeps, he sleeps in front of a 60" flat screen plasma. When he gardens, he uses his industrial sized John Deere tractor. He is not the type to spend just to spend, but he is always willing to invest a little more for quality, knowing that it will save him time and money in the long run. Respecting the views of our financier, Dan and I looked for a venue that offered us the same benefit.

Coupled with my dad's views on quality were the stories I had heard of disappointed brides who threw extravagant weddings with lots of extras. Regardless of how successful the event was, they were always disappointed in the end. They griped that every last detail they had put into their event had gone unnoticed or unappreciated by their guests. I will never forget hearing about a wedding where the bride spent a lot of money for elaborate centerpieces only to have a guest remove the arrangement from the table because it blocked his view of the other guests.

Another bride upgraded her wedding to include pink sashes that wrapped beautifully around the back of her chairs. The sashes not only served the purpose of holding down the slip-cover, but they also matched the rest of the wedding décor. Unfortunately, for her, they also resembled the sashes worn by many Miss America contestants. By the end of the night, a few gentlemen who had enjoyed one too many drinks had taken them off the chairs and wrapped them over their shoulders as if running their own personal pageant. To top it off they had taken a black marker and written across the sash what they must have thought was their crowning achievement.

These stories always brought me back to Coco Chanel's ritual: Before she left the house, the style icon removed one piece of her ensemble to avoid the faux-pas of wearing too many accessories. The same was going to be true of our wedding. We would go for quality, not quantity.

After a long search, we found the perfect match, a place that fulfilled my father's love for high quality and my desire for a venue that would keep me from having to accessorize. The venue was a mansion on Newport's fancy Bellevue Avenue. The mansion offered a beautiful ballroom, polished hardwood floors, gilded walls and mirrors reflecting the amazing view of the ocean. The ballroom was clearly designed for a wedding; it was not a confer-ence room by day and wedding venue by night. Therefore, we would not need to spend a lot of time or money transforming the location into the wedding site of our dreams. Either Ava Astor had an amazing interior decorator or she should have become one herself.

The mansion was more expensive to rent than your typical wedding venue. This was a concern for us as much as it is for any bride. This concern was offset by the panoramic ocean view, which provided the perfect backdrop during our outdoor cocktail hour and while seated in the ballroom. We had no need for special lighting or decorative upgrades. The plethora of hydrangea bushes, which were in full bloom during our reception, complimented the fresh cut hydrangea centerpieces on each table. The mansion had a beautiful veranda and garden for an outdoor cocktail hour; however, there would be no added expense if rain required us to use one of the other rooms. The quality of the venue saved us from incurring additional expenses. We did not need the usual personalized confetti, elaborate ice sculptures, PowerPoint presentations, or other distractions.

In the end, we chose a perfect venue: nothing needed to be added and nothing needed to be taken away.

The Guest List

The Perfect Number

What is the *perfect* number?

Ten seems to be the perfect number when being asked to rank someone or something in order of preference. What baby boomer doesn't remember the 1979 movie "10" starring Bo Derrick?

A mathematician will tell you, a perfect number is "one whose proper divisors add up to the number itself."

The perfect number on a test score is 100.

My perfect hair color is L'Oreal 5G.

What is the perfect number of guests for a wedding reception?

We *thought our perfect number was 170.*

My *number changed after the Engagement party.*

Why I ever put myself in the position of having to complete a major home improvement project in such a short time I will never know. I was out of my mind crazy that summer helping the kids find a wedding venue and working on the new addition in preparation for the October Engagement party. I would be on the phone inquiring about delivery of delayed kitchen appliances while calls were coming through from the caterer I had hired to help me plan the event.

I must digress for a moment and take the opportunity to confess something I did that bothers me to this day. (Although given the occasion to do it over, I would commit the very same sin.) I worked well with and appreciated everyone who worked on our renovation. They were extremely sympathetic to my situation and did their best to work together to be done in time for the celebration. I have learned through painful experience of having worked with contractors, however, that if they think the party is scheduled for October 10th, they have until the night of October 9th to complete their work. I knew if I had given them the correct party date, I would have a plumber, electrician, tile guy and painter all walking out the back door, as my invited guests were walking in the front door.

Therefore, I lied. From the start, I told these wonderful, hard working men that the party was two weeks earlier than the actual date. I always made sure that copies of the invitation were not visible. I made phone calls to the caterer and rental company from my cell phone outside the house. I often wonder if the workmen were aware of my game.

The project was completed on schedule. The fall was proving to be a continuation of summer as things moved along towards Columbus Day weekend.

Katie and Dan were excited about the party in honor of their engagement. We casually discussed inviting around fifty guests, focusing on their friends from high school and college. After years of hosting large pasta dinners for school sports teams, I felt confident I could handle a more formal home party within that range.

Ring . . . ring

"Hey, Matt, great to hear from you. Are you stuck in traffic and need some company?"

"A question?"

"Yup, Katie has invited a few friends from Chicago to the party. You know . . . Kate, Joan and Teri."

"They know a few of *your* friends? That's great, Matt."

"Oh, you would like to bring them home for the weekend? You mean the weekend of the Engagement party?"

"Um . . . um . . . sure, Matt. Any friend of yours is a friend of mine. Hey, I'm just glad you can make it home. Later."

Ring . . . ring . . . ring

"Nicole . . . Hi! You skipping class? OH . . . I'm just kidding. Are you looking forward to coming home for the Engagement party?"

"I know it is your mid semester break weekend. Don't you remember? That's why we planned the party for that weekend."

"I know you always bring your roommate and friends home for break. Do they realize it's going to be a bit crazy and that they will be attending an Engagement party?"

"I know . . . I know . . . of course they can come. Heck, they are becoming a part of the family anyway!"

Ring . . . ring . . . ring . . . ring

"Hi, sis! Long time no chat! You surviving travel soccer? Got those college applications filled out?"

"You've changed your mind?"

"The whole family can make it? He'd like to bring his girlfriend?"

"Hey that's great! Can you pick Mom up on your way to the party?"

Ring . . . ring . . . ring . . . ring . . . "We are unable to answer the phone right now . . ."

I knew the guest list was growing. I put my head in the sand and left it there. Now where did I put the painter's phone number?

The warm dry month of September transitioned into a gorgeous October 1st, 2nd, 3rd, 4th and 5th. Then the rain came. Not just rain: torrential rain. It was a leaf blowing, wind whipping, bone chilling nasty nor'easter that started on Friday night and lasted until Monday morning. By Sunday, the day of the party, the basement was flooded and the septic system stressed to the max!

I must have been especially good that year (shy of lying to the workmen) as the heavens lightened up for the six hours it took to get eighty-six people down the driveway, fed and back to their cars.

When the time came to send out the Save the Date cards, I was a wiser woman. Katie and I had begun to realize that although the reception venue offered seating for 170, perhaps a smaller number of guests would work better in the room. Determined to be more in control of the guest list for the wedding and knowing Katie and I had concerns for the allotted space, I adjusted my guest list and sent out cards committing to 150 guests, forgoing the 170 guests we had originally planned on inviting. I did not want to find ourselves in the same position at the wedding as I did at the Engagement party. I did not want to have the day arrive with no place to dance, and cocktails served in the ballroom.

I knew Katie and Dan's priorities for the reception were close friends and family . . . , and lots of dancing. One hundred and fifty guests would grant them both of those wishes.

A list was created inviting guests who were certain to attend.

I felt good about myself. I was happy we held the Engagement party. It turned out to be a wonderful afternoon with lots of laughter. It gave us the opportunity to meet many of Katie and Dan's friends whom we had heard so much about. It was a wonderful prelude to what was to come the following summer in Newport. At the same time, I was certain that I had learned a valuable lesson about controlling the guest list for the wedding.

I felt *very* good about myself.

June arrived, along with the response cards.

Our perfect number of 170 that I pared down to 150 was now changing daily. My life became one of standing at the mailbox praying for only positive responses.

"Katie . . . sit down," I said during an evening phone conversation. "We are now under 140 guests!"

"Under 140 guests? We invited 170!"

"No, Katie, I thought we talked about inviting 150 guests."

"No, Mom, we talked about inviting 170 guests, with the hope of ending up with around 150 guests."

I felt terrible. I knew this was my fault. I knew she was disappointed. I suggested sending out a few more invitations, but my suggestion hung in the air. For a time, there was a gray cloud hovering over our conversations.

As the wedding approached and we began working on table seating, I sensed Katie relaxing. Just as we realized earlier that the ballroom showed better when not filled to capacity, the ability to seat eight guests rather than ten guests at some tables simply worked better. Doing so still did not take away from the dance floor.

The day of the wedding, there was not a cloud in the gorgeous blue sky. After a cocktail hour by the water, the doors opened into a magnificent dining hall sparkling with crystal and lighted by chandeliers. People sat comfortably at tables blooming with beautiful Newport hydrangeas.

Best of all, we could all dance. And we did. Everyone!

Our perfect number was 136.

My Mother the Bouncer

If asked, any bride or groom-to-be could tell you whom they would invite to their wedding. They would know who would bring a date and who would come alone. What they might have trouble with is guessing the number of guests their parents would want to invite or, in my case, not invite. In college I always watched as bouncers clicked away while people entered and left the bar. I wondered if they were really keeping count or just trying to appease the people waiting in line outside. Was the fire department really going to stop by and check on how many people occupied the bar? My mother was not going to take that risk when it came to our wedding day!

We had picked a venue that held 170 guests in one room, and roughly 210 guests if you were willing to put the overflow in a side room. We thought that it would not be polite to put people in an overflow room so we decided to keep our guest list at 170.

Fortunately, my parents' belief was that since it was *our* wedding our guests came first, and they graciously cut guests from their list. This left us with the perfect number 170, or so I thought.

Newport is not only a popular tourist spot in the summer but is also home to many famous tennis and golf tournaments. After calling the Newport Tourism center, we realized that the weekend of our wedding was sandwiched between two popular summer events. We could not have jumped into the car and driven to Rhode Island any faster. Within one weekend we visited roughly 16 hotels in Newport and the surrounding area, and returned with a list of hotel contacts, prices and rules that applied to each hotel block.

On the ride home we narrowed our choices down to four hotels and were ready to make our Save the Date cards. My mom had been wonderful in collecting the names and addresses of all of the guests who were to be invited and my dad was nice enough to enter them into an Excel spreadsheet. I didn't have to do anything except select what color paper my Save the Date would be mounted on and what size ribbon should go around it.

Within two weeks, the Save the Date cards were in the mail detailing the date of our upcoming wedding. Despite some people's fears that we had sent out the Save the Date too soon, I knew we had done everything just right. Now we wouldn't have to worry about any of our guests being stuck without a hotel room in Newport or having to pay extremely over-priced rates for rooms because we waited until the last minute. We were all set. In fact, we had everything done so fast I never stopped to look at the guest list.

The months went by and my mom kept contacting the hotels to see who had reserved rooms. This not only let her know who she had to contact to hurry up and book a room, but it was also a great heads up on who planned on attending the wedding. According to my mother's feedback, it looked like we were going to have a full house.

As winter turned into spring it was time to send out the wedding invitations. Within a few short days we started to receive our reply cards. As expected, most of our guests replied 'yes.' Of course there were a few guests who could not attend. Our priest and our nun would not be able to join us along with a few distant cousins. This was working out perfectly. Then I got the panicked phone call from my mom. It looked like we were going to have fewer than 140 guests!

How could this have happened? No matter how hard I tried, I could not figure out how 170 minus our "sorry we will not be able to attend" reply cards came out so low. Was my mom missing some reply cards, or was she just being pessimistic?

None of the above. After seeing the ballroom at Astors she felt that to invite 170 guests would be too risky. What if everyone had said yes? Based on experience I knew she was right. When a venue could accommodate 170 guests it meant you could fit 170, but not comfortably. With that being said, I knew the 20% rule. If you invited 170 guests you could expect about 150 to attend. My mom had made up her mind not to risk an overflow and decided to play bouncer by only sending out invitations to 150.

At first I was furious. I was worried that the room would look empty with only 135 people. How was I going to explain this to Dan? Was there enough time to consider a B list? How did this happen?

A few weeks later Dan and I returned to Astors to see the ballroom set up for a wedding. While there, we were horrified to see how close the tables actually were when you had 17 tables of 10 guests each. As I looked at the cramped room my anger towards my mom subsided. Later that day as I looked at the guest list I realized that everyone both Dan and I knew and loved would be at the wedding. It was at this moment that I fully forgave my mother.

It became even clearer the night of the wedding how perfect the number actually was. Before dinner even started our guests were up and dancing. Shy of a short break to eat dinner, the dance floor stayed full the entire night. Had we invited 170 guests the room would not have allowed everyone room to dance, and we had a guest list of dancers.

My mom had played the role of bouncer well.

Communications Upgrade

Going Wireless . . . And a Few Dropped Calls

Communication is the most important component of wedding planning.

You can have the best ideas, have accomplished the most important task, and have all the details planned out, but if you don't communicate well (and that includes listening) you run the risk of acting on wrong information, making the wrong decision and worse . . . duplicating efforts.

* * * * * * * * * * * *

Communication Requires an Upgrade

Before Dan proposed to Katie, the contact list on my cell phone consisted of five family members and two close friends. Before Dan proposed, only three of the five family members ever called me on my cell phone. My two friends only called me at home.

And that was fine with me. When I leave the house for an appointment or to run errands, I focus on doing just that. Besides, I do not enjoy listening to others talk on their phone in public, and I don't want them listening to me.

I was waiting in line at my favorite coffee shop one afternoon, trying to hold strong against buying the 570 calorie Classic Coffee Cake to go with my boring medium black coffee, half regular, half decaf, when a familiar chime came from my multi-purpose, what some people would refer to as a mini-overnight, handbag. Startled, I looked around to be sure it really was my phone before I began digging to find it. The stationary shop was calling to let me know that the proof for the Save the Date cards had arrived and I could stop by at any time to look at it. Such timing! I paid for my coffee (and coffee cake) and walked over to see the proof.

I did not remember providing my cell phone number to the stationary store when ordering the Save the Date cards. But I was happy to be saving the time of having to run this errand later.

Leaving the coffee shop, I noticed a number of young adults talking on their cell phones. Several customers were hunched over small tables, communicating on their laptops. The café looked like the waiting area of an airport terminal.

I suppose by middle age one has to find a reason to dig in and learn new technology. (Or learn how to use it better.) Holding the title, Mother of the Bride, gave me that motivation. I was about to plan a wedding, using the services of an industry staffed more by Katie's generation than my own. If I wanted a quick response from the individuals helping me plan the wedding, I had to be at the other end of a cell phone or computer.

My communication began with an upgrade.

While planning the wedding, I got into the habit of providing my *cell phone* number to vendors and immediately entering their numbers into my cell phone. Now I could address any issue or question while out of the house, rather than coming home to a message and needing to call the vendor back. Often, being available to provide information to a vendor on my cell phone saved time in the delivery of an ordered product or service.

I was surprised and pleased with the many things I accomplished using my *laptop* and the *Internet*. My first instinct was that planning a wedding would require a personal touch. And it did, further down the line. Initially, however, I was able to do a great deal of research from home.

I found that communicating with vendors using the Internet had many benefits. E-mail is a quick and easy way to receive contract documents and pricing, and it provides the perfect medium for documenting, in writing, discussion points and promises made by vendors. Communicating with a vendor online, rather than by phone, gave me time to think through concerns and questions in a logical and non-emotional manner. Unlike snail mail, the vendor received my information in moments. Unlike using a phone, I did not have to worry about the vendor being free to take my call. My message was always received.

And the biggest plus to using my computer? Corresponding through e-mail allowed me to work during those long sleepless nights, when a phone call would not be appropriate or appreciated!

Despite the wonders of technology, however, my communication was not perfect.

* * * * * * * * * * *

Speaking English (in the United States) Is a Very Important Part of Communication

Picking up my Mother of the Bride dress after final alterations, I noticed something odd as the sales woman wrestled my ensemble into a protective bag.

"What are those things sewn into my top?" I asked her.

She looked at me knowingly, but quickly excused herself to locate the seamstress.

"They're boobs!" said the seamstress in an unfamiliar accent (who, by the way, only takes cash for her services).

"But I didn't ask for boobs!" I replied, thankful that I had made the decision to stay on my Hormone Replacement Therapy until after the wedding.

"You must have boobs. Big Boobs. Make you look sexy!" she insisted, cupping her own chest and taking an *open-heart* yoga pose.

Ah . . . the pose. Yes, I had seen that pose at my final fitting, and I remember a conversation she had with herself in her native language. I also remember being aware that she was shaking her head sadly as she fit my beautiful black silk organza top to my rather pint size chest. But fabric boobs? Who knew?

"But I don't want boobs!" I insisted. "They have to come out!"

I was panicking, wondering what changes would now be needed to my top to adjust for the pocket of air created by removing the fabric.

Out came the "boobs" and I was back in the dressing room once again, now late for *my* yoga class. The thought of being pinned one more time, and having to return to pick up the dress was just too much.

Fortunately, the top was not that bad . . . with a little help from Victoria's Secret.

* * * * * * * * * * * *

Communication is a Two Way Street; Except in the Wedding Industry

We were well into the decision-making and commitment process of planning the wedding before I realized that the wedding industry used **my** technique of "Only Answer the Question." The skill in wedding planning comes when you learn to ask the *right* question.

When the dust settled from lining up a church, reception venue, caterer, band, photographer, florist and limousines, I began going "under the covers."

Calling the caterer to set up a date for the tasting I asked, "My husband was wondering what table wine you will serve during the meal?"

"Oh, you want wine provided at each table?" replied the caterer.

"You bet!" I replied.

"Well, you have two options. You can bring in your own wine to be served tableside. If you bring your own wine, we do apply a corkage fee to the invoice. Or we can provide the wine and charge you by the bottle."

"But we agreed on a price for open bar. I think we're all set," I said confidently.

"Well, no. If you want wine served at the table there is an additional charge per bottle."

"Let me see if I have this right. If you serve wine tableside during dinner, we pay an additional fee per bottle. If we require the guests, who would like to enjoy a glass of wine with their dinner, to stand in a long line while their meal chills, that is covered under the open bar?"

Her answer was silence.

Well, that's a gotcha, I thought.

While making follow up phone calls, I discovered:

☞ The contract price for the band did not cover the cocktail hour.

☞ The photographer needed additional hours (at an additional charge) due to the amount of time between the ceremony and reception.

☞ The reduced pricing offered to us on blocked rooms at our favorite and most convenient (yet expensive) hotel was only valid with a minimum of 15 rooms booked for the weekend. If the minimum number of bookings fell short, we were responsible for the difference on the room charges. In addition, the use of one of their party rooms for a catered function such as a rehearsal dinner, brunch, or bridal luncheon was also required. We learned this critical information after the Save the Date cards, listing preferred hotels, had been mailed.

* * * * * * * * * * *

Communicating Relieves Stress

We were in countdown mode. In just two weeks I would be watching the heavy vestibule doors open and my bride and her father walk arm in arm down a very long aisle as the organist filled the church with the flamboyant sound of "Trumpet Voluntary."

Little did I know that up until the time the doors opened, the wedding guests would be sitting in a massive cathedral-like church in complete silence.

Or, that the wedding coordinator would be calling the limo driver seven minutes before Katie was to walk down the aisle and telling him to keep driving . . . the organist had not arrived.

Or that, come to find out, the organist had no intention of showing up before the ceremony was to begin. He had played at ceremonies a hundred times and had it down to a science. He was confident. I was a wreck. **I** had forgotten to ask the important question, "How long do you provide music before the ceremony?"

That was an upgrade.

Alert: Code Orange

While watching a famous talk show one day, I was fascinated when I heard one of the hosts explain how she spoke in code. Her friends and family knew that when she said "my feet hurt" it meant that she was uncomfortable with the topic of conversation and they needed to change the subject before she got upset. This was one of the best ideas I had ever heard! It allowed the person who was distressed to express their feelings to those around them without having to discuss the topic further. A few years later while planning my wedding, this concept became a lifesaver in many ways.

Everyone has heard someone say, "If you don't want my opinion don't ask for it." This rule applies at all times, except during the year of an engagement. As I quickly found out when someone heard the news that I was engaged, it made them feel as if they should offer something in return—their opinion for our wedding day. From venues and dates to cakes and linens I heard what everyone thought, like it or not.

Early on in the wedding planning stages I realized opinions were pouring in faster than the wedding bills my parents were receiving, and I knew my mom and I would need a code of our own. We required a system that was effective and effortlessly communicated in order to stop ourselves and others from putting their foot in their mouth. We adopted a code that was popular at the time. It was the code used by Homeland Security to alert the public to the likelihood of a terrorist attack. We simply applied their system to the likelihood of a bridezilla attack or mother of the bride meltdown. As the safety of those around us depended greatly on our emotional stability, we used the code to alert each other to avert an impending catastrophe.

Our code was straightforward. Code Green meant everything was going great while Code Yellow meant the subject at hand shouldn't be discussed at the current moment, but was best discussed at a later time. Both colors rarely came up in conversation. Code Blue may have saved my marriage and many friendships. It was a signal that we were not alone so conversations should be kept to the basics and opinions or gossip were best saved for a later date. I hate to think of how many hurt feelings we would have caused unintentionally for the sake of a little venting if it weren't for Code Blue.

Code Orange meant there was a high risk of a potential bridal meltdown. A classic example was the 16th time I was asked if I realized that July was the height of hurricane season. I simply had to say orange, and my mom would politely step in and thank the person for kindly bringing this to our attention . . . again.

You may wonder how we utilized the code yet hid what we were doing from those around us. I couldn't respond orange to the 16th person who mentioned hurricanes and not have them question my intelligence. However, I could mention that I loved their orange handbag or had considered an October wedding but didn't want to make my bridesmaids wear orange dresses and my mom would pick up on the color. By the time the wedding rolled around my mom and I were so good at the code that I could have said I was having pumpkin pie at the wedding instead of cake and my mom would pick up on the fact that pumpkins were orange and I needed an out.

The final and most important code was Code Red. This code was a clear sign of trouble ahead. It was a cry to get me out of the current situation discretely and immediately! This was often used when friends and family asked me the lowest of questions. Was I considering losing weight for my wedding—not because they thought I had to of course—they were just curious? What size was my wedding dress, and I didn't have to worry about telling them, as they understood that wedding dress sizes were smaller than normal clothing sizes. Oh, and the ultimate example of bad taste in questions: How much was this wedding costing my parents? They only asked, they said, so they could start planning for their own wedding. Yes, these tacky and insensitive questions were asked with the best of intentions . . . and when I smiled and replied I thought the wedding was leaving my parents in the red, my mom knew it was time to pull me away.

Having a code will not only help you with unwanted opinions, but it can also save you in the planning stages of a wedding when you are trying to figure out which vendors you would like to use . . . and who needs to be cut from the list. All of the vendors we worked with were wonderful, but the road to finding them was not always smooth. This is when the code became a blessing. As vendors were pushing their opinion on what they felt was perfect for our wedding, my mom and I could simply use the alert system, know what it meant, and move on to the next vendor on our list.

Having recently graduated from college, I was sensitive to the fact that my friends would not want to spend a lot of money on hotel rooms. So I compiled a list of less expensive hotels that would better fit my friends' budgets, and my mom and I set off to Newport to check them out and block some rooms. Our first stop was at a cute hotel beside a main road. It did not offer much privacy, but it looked nice and clean from the outside and we had been informed that it offered reasonable pricing. We went inside and were greeted by a dirty lobby and a less than friendly gentleman sporting long unkempt dreadlocks and one too many piercings. We had already made an appointment to see the rooms and felt guilty turning heel without even the slightest explanation.

My mom grabbed my arm and pointed out the lovely orange carpet. I looked down to see a multi-colored rug and took the hint.
I mentioned that I thought I had left my keys in the car. We
excused ourselves to go check and as I quickly drove away from
the hotel my mom broke out the hand sanitizer she kept stashed
in her purse.

It worked wonders at all of the parties we attended during the
year of the engagement as well. Often during these events both
sides of the family were attending, and while as the bride you
know the background on all of the guests, your poor mother is
left clueless. There were multiple occasions when my mom accidentally broached a touchy topic with the wrong women. The
worst incident took place at a party when my mom mentioned
how ridiculous it was that women actually had plastic surgery for
weddings, not realizing that a woman in the room had recently
had Botox injections for ours. Quickly, I pointed to the red orien-
tal and asked if it was the same shade as the one in my parents'
living room and my mother changed the subject from Botox to
interior decorating.

The code method worked both ways. There were often times
I would call my mom to ask about pricing or additional items for
the wedding and my dad was standing nearby. When she mentioned the bluebird that was on the birdfeeder I knew I should
e-mail her my questions later. When I called my mom to discuss
the bridesmaids' gifts and my sister was standing nearby, my
mom said that she had to go to the bathroom and I knew that it
was a code yellow. It was something we would discuss later. The
code helped keep plenty of secrets between the two of us that
year.

You may wonder why we didn't just say, "Now isn't a good
time" or "Let's change the subject" or honestly tell our vendors
how we were feeling. But in the emotionally charged wedding
world, saying *Now isn't a good time", "Let's change the subject"* or
"I don't like this invitation" just piques everyone's interest and leads

to more discussion. Rather than getting you out of trouble, these statements tend to drag you into more. And the last thing we were looking for the year of the wedding was more trouble!

FAQ

Jeopardy

I have a dear friend who is considering a move to South Carolina to avoid the New England winters and live closer to her daughters. I wish her the best, and yet I pray every night that she will change her mind and stay put. She is organized and thorough, always staying one step ahead of life. For example, she keeps a shoebox containing invitations and notes from weddings she has attended, so that she will be prepared when the time comes to plan a wedding for her own girls.

Heading out to the garden to take advantage of a cool summer morning, I was interrupted by a phone call from Katie and Dan's "first choice" reception site. They were calling to say they needed a deposit to hold the venue for our preferred date. I had contacted Katie and Dan what felt like hundreds of times to confirm their decision about booking this particular venue. A hundred times I received an excited, "You bet!" But I still could not pull the trigger.

I walked the kitchen floor for an hour screwing up my courage to commit to the venue. I only saw the word **enormous** floating through my mind. I knew it was inevitable. I placed a return call to the venue's contact to give her my most valued ten-digit number, expiration date and three-digit security code. As I hung up the phone, my friend pulled in the driveway.

"I was hoping you would book Newport!" she said, anticipating that the wedding would make for a great weekend getaway.

"Will you be providing transportation for the guests from the hotel to the church and reception?"

No answer.

"Any thoughts on the rehearsal dinner?"

Blank stare.

"Have you looked into booking hotels?"

The timing of her rapid-fire questioning stunk. The guidance and advice that she provided over the next several months was invaluable.

My friend's curiosity on wedding details was not abnormal. In fact, I began to discover that every time I mentioned Katie's upcoming wedding in public I was met with a barrage of questions. Not yet aware of all the decisions I had facing me and not having answers to all these questions made me nervous.

From the moment Katie became engaged, I felt like I was a contestant on *Jeopardy*. I was fielding information on a regular basis, often not certain where it fit into the planning of a wedding.

Answer: A box filled with crinkled paper, in the bridal colors, containing a bottle of local wine, an opener, cheese, crackers, nuts and Tylenol.

Question: What is a welcome gift?

Answer: This item is small, cylindrical, and requires the Mother of the Bride to leave her comfortable seat during the wedding ceremony.

Question: What is a unity candle?

Answer: It requires a technical degree to produce, makes the guests laugh and the bride cringe, and takes away from dance time?

Question: What is a PowerPoint Presentation of the Bride and Groom as children?

Answer: The perfect Father's Day gift for the Father of the Bride.

Question: What are dance lessons?

Answer: Couture.

Question: What fashion expression used in the wedding industry adds $$$$ to the bottom line of the cost of the Bridal Gown?

And now . . . *Final Jeopardy*

Answer: Upgraded linens, chair covers, table wine, wedding cake and cutting fees.

Question: What wedding reception costs are not included in the original quote?

As if all of this questioning weren't enough to add antacids to my daily diet, the people who scared me the most were those individuals who had attended a wedding, but had never *put on* a wedding. Personally, I feel if you have an *opinion* from having attended a wedding, you are welcome to keep it to yourself. I was on the look out for people with *experience*.

Paul and I married young. In fact, we were the first of our college peer group to walk down the aisle, and we were subjected to many *opinions* by well-intentioned friends.

"I'll never make my ushers wear a tuxedo!"

"I'm keeping my bridal party small, just my two sisters!"

"No way am I having a big church wedding!"

Funny how they all succumbed to wedding traditions when it was their turn to walk down the aisle!

Memories of my own wedding planning came rushing back as I began planning for Katie's. Once again, I felt intimidated because so much involved in planning a wedding had changed.

It took time for me to become comfortable with how Katie and Dan's wedding choices were taking shape: the distance, the unknown expense, the new traditions. As I gained confidence, I began enjoying conversations with others, seeking out those who could say, "Been there . . . done that." I sorted through information, considering ideas that applied to our situation and weeding out suggestions that did not.

I have to give Katie credit. For a girl who never talked about weddings before becoming engaged, she sure had her head on straight once we started to plan. From the start, Katie was not prone to listening to whirlwind advice or opinions of others. She was *Not Her Mother's Daughter* when it came to being intimidated by others. She simply stayed focused on what was important to Dan and to her.

I may have been the one who carried the three ring binder at planning and vendor meetings. But in the end, it was Katie who truly had the game plan. It didn't happen overnight, but eventually the day came when I had more answers than questions. And what a great day that was.

Chicken & Rice

My mother had warned me that it would not be easy to be the first of my friends to get married. "Everyone will have an opinion, but no experience," she said. Although known for being a downer at times, she hit the nail on the head with that comment. Everyone and their mother had a suggestion on what would make my wedding perfect. I was traumatized to learn the menu was the biggest concern of my closest friends and random strangers. People wanted to know if we were having steak or lobster, if it was going to be a buffet or plated dinner, and what they would be served for dessert. My friends from NYC were shocked when I did not know what a Venetian Room was. After all, how can someone who lives on candy NOT have heard of a Venetian Room?

What everyone seemed to forget was that I was not a foodie, as a direct result of my mother's simple cooking. Salmon never entered the house because the smell made everyone sick and when my mom tried to feed us white fish it had to be buried in butter and breadcrumbs, thus defeating the purpose of its health benefits. The one night my dad tried to get creative and add garlic to the standard Sunday night steak, my sister vomited on the dinner table. To be fair to the family I have to admit that I was the worst and I do remember a few lonely dinners when the rest of my family enjoyed lobster on the deck and I had to eat inside at the bar because I started to gag when I joined them outside.

We just aren't a family of connoisseurs. As you can imagine, when the time came to select menu options for the reception, we found ourselves out of our comfort zones.

While my mom was more Chef Boyardee and less Wolfgang Puck, I will give her credit for making sure we all sat down and had dinner as a family every night. Mom cooked chicken and rice for dinner Monday through Saturday, with the exception of the summer when we had chicken and corn on the cob. On Sunday nights we had steak, but I refused to eat steak, so I had chicken or pasta on those nights too.

Despite Dan's hesitation (he has a lot of Italian friends), Mom and I agreed that the focus on the meal at a wedding was over-rated. Her Irish grandmother always said, "If you keep them busy with liquid refreshments, they won't know what they are eating." Besides, we were focusing on a good band! But we couldn't ignore that nagging feeling in the back of our minds telling us that to some guests the reception would be made or lost on the food choices.

Our caterer was our saving grace when it came to our final decision. I wanted the food at our wedding to be special. Too often at events I had organized, beef entrées were not to the liking of the guests due to the volume of people served. Yet, as I thought back to all of those chicken and rice dinners, I feared it would be too simple. As I explained my feelings of baked chicken with no seasoning and a side of rice pilaf to our caterer she started to laugh. After rattling off a list of various ways the chicken could be prepared and showing me pictures of a variety of ways chicken can be presented on the plate, my concerns started to fade and I was sold on the entrée for my wedding. It was simple; we would be having fancy chicken and rice! It was the perfect compromise between my desire for a well prepared meal and my guests' well developed palates.

When our wedding day arrived everything seemed to fall into place. Cocktail hour ended and we moved into the dining room.

Dan and I got up to dance. My mom and I didn't know if we should laugh or cry when we saw what happened next. The band kicked up the music and everyone joined us on the dance floor. As we saw the chicken and rice beautifully displayed on the plates set at everyone's table my mom threw me a quizzical look across the dance floor. Our one hope for the wedding had been to make it a huge party where everyone danced the night away. But we couldn't believe it as we watched the food sit at the tables and everyone ignoring it as they continued to dance!

As the night progressed everyone eventually sat down (if only for a few minutes) to eat their dinner and listen to the best men and maid of honor give their speeches. Between the amazing caterers we worked with and our decision to go with what we knew we liked (rather than what others told us we should like), everything worked out. It not only worked out, but everyone loved it. What's more important is that we loved it, and, in the end, that is what matters.

You can please some of the people all of the time.
And you can please all of the people some of the time.
But you cannot please all of the people all of the time.

Project
Management 101

Supplies for the Mother of the Bride

Supplies for
the Bride

Wedding Couture

The Promise

I must admit that secretly, while planning Katie's wedding, my major concern was, "WHAT WILL I WEAR?"

Still in high school, Katie woke up startled one night. Meeting her in the hallway, I asked what was wrong. "It was the worst!" she said. "I just had a dream that you showed up at my wedding wearing a black pantsuit!"

I can't say her dream (or nightmare) was unfounded. I live in black and favor black accessories.

I also live in pants. I refuse to wear stockings, with or without control top. I find them too uncomfortable and itchy. I have middle-aged legs that are acceptable when sporting a tan in the summer. However, as soon as I put my summer whites away after Labor Day, I put my bare legs under cover into slacks . . . **Black Slacks!**

That very day Katie had taken me shopping to find an outfit to wear to her brother's college graduation. She sent me into a dress shop to begin my search and said she would meet me shortly. Twenty minutes later, she found me in a dressing room trying on . . . a black pantsuit. Rolling her eyes, she handed me a teal sheath dress with small yellow appliqués. I looked lovely. I bought the dress and received a startling compliment from my son at graduation. He made my day . . . twice.

Ten years later, after rejecting several Mother of the Bride dresses, the saleswoman to whom we gave strict instructions not to show us anything in black, appeared with a gorgeous two-piece ensemble. The top, a black silk organza, complimented a floor length black trumpet skirt with white appliqués. "Mom, it is so you!" said Katie without hesitation. "You have to try it on."

"I promised you I would not walk down the aisle in black at your wedding and I am keeping that promise," I said firmly.

"You don't have to buy it," Katie said. "Just try it on."

It was perfect. True, the color was comfortable, but so was the style. I bought it along with special order jewelry created with sparkling crystals and pearls, and a crystal embroidered black and white clutch.

We looked at some beautiful Mother of the Bride gowns that day. The selection of flowing fabrics, shimmering colors in fashionable designs, were endless. The dresses were exactly what one would expect to see being worn by the proud mother as she walked down the aisle. They just weren't *me*.

I wanted to conform to expectations. It was Katie's day to shine and I did not want my dress to draw attention away from her, whether for a good choice or a bad one. I wanted Katie to be proud of me.

There comes a time when we begin to appreciate that what we feel most comfortable wearing is not going to be high fashion; or in this case, the traditional Mother of the Bride gown. Katie knew that feeling good about our dresses on the day of the wedding meant a great deal to both of us. Rather than insisting I be limited to a bridal theme, she allowed me to choose what I would be comfortable wearing on her wedding day. I felt that Katie put aside her preference towards any fashion choices she may have had. To some this may seem insignificant. To me it meant everything.

I wore the dress that Katie and I chose together and never felt prettier. Thank you, Katie.

Going Green

My mom and I have always had a running joke that she was not allowed to wear black at my wedding. While I was growing up my mom always wore black when she wanted to dress up or feel confident about an outfit. She had black pantsuits for work, black dresses for special occasions and black sweats for lounging. While in high school I feared that my mom would show up at my wedding wearing her traditional black uniform. However, as the wedding approached and the costs started to add up, my feelings toward my mother's dress changed. I needed a partner in crime.

While shopping for a mother of the bride dress one weekend I was horrified to hear that brides actually thought they should have a say in what their mother and the groom's mother should wear to the wedding. The saleswoman told us of one bride who had her future mother-in-law in tears as they tried on dresses. I had struggled enough trying to choose the bridesmaids dresses, and ended up having to call in reinforcements (my sister). I certainly was not going to try to choose an outfit for my mom or anyone else.

We had looked around the store and we had seen a few lovely dresses that we thought might work. With our arms full we headed to the dressing room. After trying on a few selections we were both becoming frustrated. The gowns either looked too dowdy or they left my mom looking like an uncomfortable teenager in her prom dress. We just couldn't find the happy medium we were looking for.

All of a sudden, the saleswoman came around the corner carrying a dress that seemed to come out of nowhere. It was exactly what we were trying to avoid . . . it was perfect. When my mom put it on, it looked amazing. My mom argued that the dress was black and she had promised not to wear black to my wedding.

I wasn't looking at the color. My mind was focused on the silk organza top and the white appliqués that ran down the trumpet skirt. This dress was expensive! I knew the cost of the dress would be compatible with my wedding dress, not only because of the material and detailed stitching, but also because the price tag was small and almost hidden. My mom thought I wanted her to buy the dress because it was so *her.* That wasn't exactly the case.

The real reason I wanted her to buy an expensive dress was due to middle child guilt. I had ordered an expensive wedding dress a few months earlier and had been experiencing sudden pangs of guilt when I was around my father. I knew that I would only wear the dress once (well, hopefully), and that he had shelled out a lot of money for it. Despite the fact that every homecoming dress and prom dress I had purchased growing up was a few dollars away from a blue light special, I still felt guilty splurging on my wedding gown. I was concerned that I would be in the doghouse with our setter Tango as soon as Dad found out how much it cost, and I knew he would find out. I would only get away with my purchase if my mom got an expensive dress too. There is safety in numbers.

While the dress looked great on my mom, and I could tell she felt comfortable in it, what made it easy to overlook the color was the cost. If she had found a great black pantsuit that put her in the doghouse with me, that would have been just fine as long as I wasn't going it alone.

When my mom finally bought the dress, I knew I was safe. She would look fantastic at the wedding, and Tango would not be having guests anytime soon. Thank you, Mom.

The Shower

A New Screenplay

It is healthy to release frustration. Unfortunately, it seems that to get the most out of that release someone or something needs to be there to receive it. We have all experienced the reality that crap flows downhill. We chuckle at the stereotypical husband/father coming home from a tough day at work, tired and stressed, only to take his irritation out on the family dog.

I introduced two dogs into our family years ago. Yet, when anyone in my family becomes irritated, they pet the dogs, find them a treat, and come looking for **MOM!**

I dreaded the bridal shower. It would be *deja vu* of preparing for proms and fussy occasions.

The screenplay for the day of the shower was written in my mind:

FADE IN:

CAR RIDE TO EVENT – MORNING

MOM (*cheerfully*)

What a beautiful day for your shower, Katie. I love your sundress.

KATIE (*perturbed*)

I'm more comfortable in the dress I bought at Banana Republic, but I know you like this one better.

MOM (*puzzled*)

Gosh, I know I said I like the dress you are wearing, but I don't remember comparing it to the Banana dress.

KATIE (*disappointed*)

I thought you said you were going to shop for a dress too. Everyone will be wearing a dress.

MOM (*hesitantly*)

Remember I told you I didn't have any luck finding a dress that I liked? You said it would be ok to wear my new pantsuit.

KATIE (*agitated*)

Well, at least it's not black. Khaki is a nice change . . . Why do you keep looking at me?

MOM (*cautiously perky*)

I just think you look so pretty. And I'm very proud of you.

KATIE (*really agitated*)

Yeah, well you're not the one who has to sit in front of a bunch of people you don't know and pretend you have a clue as to what the gift is used for.

MOM (*confidently*)

I've got you covered. If I see you waver, I'll say something . . . . .

KATIE *(firmly)*

I'll be fine. PLEASE don't say anything. Just smile (pause). When did you start wearing your hair pulled back?

MOM *(hopeful)*

Just recently. Dad likes it. What do you think?

KATIE *(no emotion)*

I'm just not used to it.

MOM *(worried)*

This sign says we still have quite a drive ahead of us. I thought you said the trip was only 45 minutes from Boston.

KATIE *(dramatically)*

No, you said that Dad said it would only be a 45-minute drive! It takes me over an hour!

FADE OUT.

The screenplay was written out in my mind word for word. My only uncertainty was whether or not **I** would get through the event gracefully.

As it turned out, there was no sequel to those stressful high school events. Here is how the scene actually played out.

Katie's bridal shower was being held in Bedford, New Hampshire, an hour's drive from Boston. With Katie now living in Boston's North End (known for its fabulous authentic Italian restaurants), Nicole and I decided to join her for a fun weekend in Bean Town. We booked ourselves into one of Boston's charming hotels near Quincy Market. Katie arrived to find us relaxing on the heavenly beds and shaking out our outfits for the next day.

The next stop was the hotel lounge to catch the running of the Kentucky Derby. Matt and several of his friends from Chicago had made their annual pilgrimage to the event seeking fun and fortune. We ordered a drink and settled into the soft leather club chairs near the Flat-Panel TV. We searched for Matt in the sea of spectators, but to no avail. After receiving a text from him informing us of his meager winnings, we headed out to experience the city.

Conversation and laughter consumed the afternoon. Winding down over dinner I brought the girls current on happenings with the extended family. Katie updated us on the next day's guest list, and we reviewed logistics as to where she would store her shower gifts.

Being in the girls' company felt so familiar, yet not really. In the past, I would have felt responsible for the success or failure of our time together. I would have worked at steering conversation in a safe direction, staying away from areas of known conflict. I would have been the pessimistic mother waiting for *the other shoe to drop*. As the night progressed I found myself feeling more relaxed: more a companion than a mother.

Was Katie feeling responsible for making sure that Nicole and I had fun? Or was she simply enjoying our company? She showed no concern over being center stage the next day.

Clearly, she was not following the story line I had written for her shower.

The drive to New Hampshire was uneventful, with Katie pointing out areas of interest along the way. It would be unusual for Nicole (or me) not to release some nervousness with the banter of possible worse case scenarios. Katie, joking in return, was seeing the humor in it all.

It was the first warm day of spring. A delightful friend of Dan's family had opened up her home to Katie. She had decorated with blue hydrangeas, Katie's wedding flower, displaying a sampling of the wedding to come. We mingled on the front lawn, not wanting to leave the welcomed sun. I began putting names with faces, and faces into categories . . . family, friends, neighbors. I shared information about the wedding, as others shared their wedding experiences.

I watched my bride as she visited with her guests. To her these were not strangers. They were her new family. They laughed about shared experiences, such as boating at a summer home and caroling at Christmas.

That night I played back the events of the weekend. It became clear to me that the screenplay in my mind needed to be archived. Katie had a new story to tell with chapters full of confidence and adventure. To say she had grown up would not give credit to the person she had become.

A needed change happened to me that weekend. Until the shower I had not found my confidence for planning such a big event. Somewhere between the engagement and the shower I had lost sight of what the wedding was all about. I completed tasks but was held back from the excitement of planning the wedding because of the uncertainty of it all. That weekend I saw in Katie the confidence I had lost. My partner on this project was a strong and determined player. I was back on track.

My new screenplay begins:

MOM

My daughter is getting married and I am so excited!

The Most Dangerous Gun

Dan is a true techie, one of the things I especially love about him. Not because he has supplied me with two mounted flat screen TVs attached to Seagate hard drives. And not because they supply us with endless DVD storage eliminating the need to dust the DVDs on the rack. It's mostly because I enjoy watching him be so passionate about something. Technology is truly a hobby that he loves and it provides him with a healthy activity occupying his free time and allowing me to enjoy my own hobbies. Only once in my life have I regretted marrying someone who is so technical. It was when Dan and I registered for our wedding gifts.

Dan had teased me endlessly about wanting to register at Best Buy and Radio Shack, but all in good fun and never seriously. While Dan realized that he wouldn't be registering for electronics he figured he would enjoy the registry process since it involved using a computer and registry gun.

Our first stop was Crate and Barrel and I couldn't wait to walk around the store and pick out items. After a brief introduction on how to register properly, we were handed our copy of the Top Ten Mistakes Couples Make When Registering and our first registry gun. Confused as to how to work the thing, Dan grabbed it from me and said he would take care of it. So off we went to register. We spent hours picking out silverware, dishes and barware, always referring to our new manual so as not to make mistakes. Dan not only entered everything into the system by using the gun, but he was also able to control the quantity without us having to scan the item several times. Once again, his passion for electronics was paying off.

While in Crate and Barrel we ran into one little problem that caused a minor disagreement between us. As a ploy to get you to register for large items, the store offers a 10% discount on any items left on your registry after the wedding. If you register for a bedroom set, for example, even though you don't expect anyone to buy it for you, you can purchase it for yourself after the wedding with a 10% discount. Dan is always looking for the next bargain and thought it would be a great idea to register for items we wanted to purchase after the wedding. I was afraid guests would be offended when they saw that we registered for such expensive gifts and decided it would be best to register only for items within a certain price range. While I trusted Dan, I kept a close eye on where he was waving that gun.

Our next stop was Bed Bath and Beyond. After struggling to keep a straight face during the important "how to choose the right bathroom towel for you" seminar, we were once again handed a registry gun and were on our way. We had a great time registering for our everyday dishes and knives and a few other fun items. Not a cook myself, Dan took control of registering for pasta strainers, spatulas and other kitchen items while I took charge of anything we would need to clean and organize our new home. All in all, it was a great day.

We registered a few months before our wedding so I didn't think we'd have many people looking at our registry, but just in case, Dan went ahead and set up our account online. Dan also took charge of monitoring our registry, leaving me free to handle other wedding tasks. I knew Dan would let me know if there were any problems.

A few weeks after we registered, my sister called me giggling about a few items that she had seen on our Bed Bath and Beyond registry. Nicole mentioned that Mom was using our wedding registry for Christmas gift ideas and suggested that she could use it as well. At this point, Nicole was dying from laughter so I quickly went online to see what was so funny.

As I scanned the registry webpage I couldn't find anything that would cause a laughing fit. I slowly scrolled down over towels and linens, dishware and closet organizers. Everything looked fine. Then I got to the bottom of the screen and there it was. *Nose hair trimmers!* Why had Dan registered for nose hair trimmers? Was he mad at me for not letting him register for more expensive items? Or had he taken the price range too seriously? Was this his idea of a joke? I kept scrolling and found other odd items too, such as a Squeezy McSqueezum for toothpaste and a mirror that magnified images 10X. What was Dan thinking? It was beginning to look like a gift registry for an over the hill birthday party. Not only did we not need these items (at least not yet), but they all cost less than $5.00. If he really wanted them he could have purchased them himself.

As my sister continued to laugh about the nose hair trimmers, I joined along with her. It *was* funny that Dan would choose to register for these items, and thankfully it was way too early for anyone outside of our family to have logged into our registry to place an order. I had plenty of time to remove them from the list.

As I was reading the description of the nose hair trimmers *"rotary style blades"* that *remove hair safely and easily* and laughing, my sister asked, "Well, who do you think bought them for you?"

My heart sank as I looked at the little box and realized that they had been purchased. I was mortified! Someone actually thought we registered for these items and had already bought them. I felt bad for the guest and mad at Dan for putting me in the position of having to find out who ordered them so I could explain. I knew I should have taken the registry gun license away from Dan when I had the chance.

I quickly contacted Bed Bath and Beyond and, after some investigation, found out that Dan had not registered for these gifts as an act of revenge. It turns out my mother was not the only one who had thought to use our registry as a Christmas list that year. My future Mother-in-Law, who is known for putting together fun and memorable family stockings, had used it as well. When she checked out with gifts from our registry, the items that would be placed in the stockings were accidentally added to our registry.

Christmas morning we all had a great laugh about the incident. Dan was happy to find his gun license wrapped under the tree.

Botox and a Broken Nose

Just the Way You Are

An unfortunate fact of life is that we do not learn from others' mistakes. To gain knowledge we must fall on our face and learn from experience. Truth be told, we never listened to our parents, and our kids never listen to us.

I also overlook common sense sometimes, even when it is staring at me in the morning mirror. That is why I made mistake after hairdo mistake during the first 40 years of my life.

Looking at old family photos recently, my stomach flipped as I found a picture of me sporting a rather short, over-permed hairdo. I would rank it my number one worst hairstyle ever; it looked like a mix between Jimmy Hendricks and Ronald McDonald. You would think that common sense would have kicked in immediately. However, I paid dearly for a permanent every four months even though I was too curly for the first month and rather ratty looking the last month. I wore that hairstyle for almost three years.

By the time the engagement was announced I had already tried every hairdo possible on my rather long face and longer neck. Thank heavens I settled on a timeless, but pleasing hairstyle. I felt comfortable knowing that when I looked back on the upcoming wedding photos, my hair would not cause me to gasp, "Oh my heavens, what was I thinking?"

My hair was the easy part.

What caused me anxiety was realizing I was a viable candidate for several youth producing cosmetic surgery options. Not only was I in the prime marketing age group for Botox and Laser treatments, **I** was the MOTHER OF THE BRIDE! I had a major role to play. I had to look my best. I would be letting Katie down if I did not take advantage of what the medical and cosmetic industry had to offer to make me look young again.

In her book, *You're Wearing That?*, Deborah Tannen writes about how important it is for a young girl to know that her mother is proud of her. Who's kidding whom? The tables have turned. Fifty is the new thirty . . . and women in middle age want our daughters to be proud of **us!**

It is no secret that beauty enhancement treatments, age reducing surgeries and advanced personal care products are all the rage. Cosmetic surgery to improve appearance and reconstructive surgery to correct defects are becoming available and affordable. (At least they appear affordable when compared to all the other wedding expenses.) I wanted them all!

Taking advantage of the local gym, come to find out, was the quickest way to bring myself up to speed on looking younger. Middle-aged women who work out are not only concerned about having a tight butt; they want to look good *coming* too. They want a great face. Not only were the women helpful in providing a quick reference to the best surgeon in the area, they also offered an up-close show and tell. Women who have had cosmetic surgery are great supporters of having cosmetic surgery. They also know that the wedding year is no time to be wishy-washy on decision-making. I was the bride's mother and I had to shine!

I was overwhelmed. Until I had started to investigate beauty treatments, I flew through my morning application of skin cream and makeup without much thought. Now I found my coffee getting cold as I stared at my sagging eyelids (so that's why I find my eye shadow under my eyebrows by mid day!), my crows feet (the product of not wearing sunglasses while lifeguarding during my college summers) and my laugh lines. How could I not have noticed the deep lines surrounding my mouth? Was I blind?

By the time I had researched and decided on my options for tapping into the fountain of youth I realized I was too late. Prior to the wedding there were showers and vendor meetings. I had not allowed myself time to factor in healing, and, heaven forbid, corrective surgery appointments to address any unforeseen reactions or "oops" results on the first attempt.

Fortunately, I had learned from suffering through bad hairdos that a drastic change before a significant event can lead to "Oh good heavens, what was I thinking?"

I invested in silk nails (still have them), a few silk peels at the dermatologist (saw no difference) and a trip to the Lancôme counter at our local mall.

Options Found in the Fountain of Youth

Hair: Highlights or Glazing
Eyebrow Waxing
Eyebrow Coloring
Eyelash Coloring
Teeth Whitening/Bleaching
Manicure
Pedicure
Nail Extensions (Silk, Acrylic, etc.)
Tanning Crèmes
Tanning Beds
Spray on Tans
Dermabrasion
Silk Peels/Chemical Peels
Botox
Restilyn
Eyelid Surgery
Face Lifts
Hair Replacement
Laser Skin Resurfacing
Permanent Eyeliner
Laser Treatment for Spider Veins
Collagen Injection
Breast Implants

And in the end, my hair looked great.

Doctor Fist

Weddings make people do dramatic things they never would have considered prior to the news of the engagement of their friend, daughter, neighbor or even themselves. The year I was engaged I heard dozens of people discuss how they would lose weight for my wedding even though they didn't need to. Friends shopped for expensive dresses for the wedding even though they couldn't afford them. People were willing to go to extremes to make sure they would look their best. I could laugh at all of this as ridiculous, but the one thing that made me cringe was when I heard people speak of plastic surgery. Thanks to a fun night with my siblings and drinking one too many Lemon Drops, I knew the one thing I would never do for my wedding, or anyone else's, was contemplate plastic surgery.

My time in Chicago was coming to an end, and I was getting ready to move back to Connecticut to be closer to Dan. I thought it would be great to have Nicole out to visit. She didn't receive an invitation to fly to Chicago that often, as my brother was not eager to have his sisters tagging along.

The weather was beautiful so we were all excited for the upcoming visit. Nicole arrived on Thursday morning and we had a great day of shopping and going out to dinner on Michigan Avenue. The next day was just as nice as we lounged on the beach. Her friend was coming into town the following morning, so we planned to have one last "siblings" night with Matt before her friend arrived. We headed over to Matt's for a quick cocktail before going out for the evening.

After finishing dinner in Chicago's Old Town we headed to a bar down the street where we met up with a few of Matt's closest friends. We had an excellent time at the bar and my sister and I enjoyed a few Lemon Drops. Somehow we ended up on Rush and Division Streets slamming down a few more drinks. Discovering that I had stolen an entire pizza from the bar, my brother thought it would be best for us to leave before we got into any real trouble.

As we started to walk home, I was convinced we were headed in the wrong direction. I stopped two rather large gentlemen and asked them if we were headed the right way. They confirmed that we were and went on their way. I must have blacked out here, but various stories have surfaced as to how these young men ended up turning around and starting the biggest fight I have ever experienced in my life. All I remember is falling down and feeling the blood running down my face as my sister yelled, "You ruined her new shirt!"

The next thing I knew I was in the emergency room with a bloody—and possibly broken—nose, and two black eyes. Three hours later the doctors confirmed that my nose was not broken. They handed me a few Extra Strength Tylenol and a list of plastic surgeons so I could schedule a follow-up visit to have the stitches removed and my nose checked for fractures. I was so happy that I hadn't broken my nose before my wedding that I let my brother convince me to go to McDonald's for a quick breakfast. This is when I realized how bad I looked.

I went up to the counter to place my breakfast order and was met with a look of horror. Confused, I told my brother I was going to go wash my hands before I ate my breakfast, as I had spent the past three hours in a germy hospital. As I entered the bathroom the cleaning lady took one look at me and fled. It was only then that I looked into a mirror for the first time. Not only was my nose swollen to three times its normal size, but both of my eyes had started to swell up and close in towards my nose. I was covered in blood and dirt and looked like I had just been in a horrible car accident.

At this point, the combination of alcohol and codeine kept me from panicking about how I would look on my wedding day, but the next morning was horrible. Not only did I have to face myself in the mirror, but I would also have to call my mom to let her know that her newly engaged daughter might have to go under the knife to straighten out a crooked nose. It wasn't going to be pretty.

True to form, my mother produced a litany of worse case scenarios on my healing. After what felt like hours I reminded her that my brother and sister were not in jail, I hadn't lost any teeth and my nose had time to heal.

A few weeks later I met with a plastic surgeon. He confirmed that my nose was not broken, but that it had fractured and would take a few months to heal completely. In the event that it did not heal correctly, I was given a list of plastic surgeons in Connecticut who could remove any fractured pieces.

The following three months truly confirmed that I would never contemplate plastic surgery. From the start, my head felt like a bowling ball and my nose would not stop bleeding. The stitches weren't supposed to get wet and since they were in the middle of my face it made showering very difficult. It was hard to breathe, and as the swelling went down it became apparent that my nose was angled in a way it wasn't prior to the punch. I started to worry that my nose would be crooked forever. My biggest fear was that I might need corrective surgery, which would bring me back to square one as far as the swelling and black eyes were concerned.

There's nothing that bothers me so much about myself that I feel I need plastic surgery. But I feel I benefited from my nose

crushing experience. It taught me that the healing process is very long and painful, and you never know the results until all of the swelling goes down. I was fortunate that when the swelling finally subsided completely my nose was still as straight as it was before the punch (not perfectly straight – but not the Leaning Tower of Pisa it was headed for either).

During the year I was engaged I heard more women young and old talk about face-lifts, Botox and boob jobs than I had ever heard in my life. Before my meeting with Dr. Fist, maybe I would have considered having some *procedures* done prior to my wedding day. But thanks to a memorable night with my siblings I learned that the road to accepting yourself the way you are is much less painful than the road to recovery after a major trauma to the body.

Details,
Details . . . and
More Details

The Round Table

Katie and Dan's engagement made me conscious of a new passage in my life. Attendance at the weddings of nieces, nephews, and children of close friends was on the horizon. At that moment, however, I was thrown right into planning a traditional wedding with very little experience to support the assignment. While out running errands, I found myself eavesdropping on strangers talking about an engagement or upcoming wedding. When my friends discussed the engagement of an individual I did not know, rather than politely smiling and responding, "Oh, that's nice," I now jumped right into the conversation with my growing list of questions.

Again I digress . . . While planning this wedding I discovered that the build-up to an engagement often has a life of its own. There are couples who *are planning to be engaged,* and by the time it happens you are just happy that now *you* can move on. Of course, there are the couples struggling with their relationship, who totally blind side you with their engagement announcement. In either case, there is such pressure today on the poor guy to be *original* with his proposal technique! Sometimes buying the perfect ring (while keeping it a surprise) and proposing at a location of memorable significance, while coordinating the *popping of the question* with a romantic sunset is an achievement in itself. Congratulations to the guys who pull it off!

But let's face it . . . regardless of whether the sun was rising or setting, or if we think the couple is destined to be together *'til death . . .* after the hugs and kisses, what women really want to know is the *where* and *when* of the upcoming wedding. A wedding requires planning, scheduling and wardrobe assessment on everyone's part!

While rushing around trying to provide just those answers for the *where* and *when* of Katie and Dan's wedding, I was naive to the importance of addressing the DETAILS. I did not comprehend at the time that the *who*, the *how*, the *why* and the *whatever* were just as important as the *where* and *when*!

In hindsight, I should have read my coffee table quality guidebook, *The Bride's Year Ahead: The Ultimate Month-by-Month Wedding Planner,* from beginning to end before taking any action. However, I did not. I began with Chapter 1.

Twelve Months Ahead: Book a reception hall or hire a caterer.

That is exactly what we were doing the afternoon Katie and I walked to the car, after touring yet another reception venue.

"Well, that place isn't going to work," I said to Katie. "They hardly have room for a **head table**, much less a decent sized **dance floor**."

What I got in return from Katie was the oddest look. Not *The Look*. I know what *The Look* means and it wasn't that. It was kind of a *What the Hell are You Talking About Look.*

I should have questioned her reaction to my assessment of the venue further but I did not. I was tired. We had just visited our fourth and last reception venue of the day. Where I always look forward to my wine with dinner, I found that the last several weeks of intense wedding planning had resulted in also looking forward to a Tanguery and Tonic (extra lime) before the wine. My mind was on the cocktail hour and I was losing focus. I quickly forgot about the head table and unlocked the car.

Time flies, especially when you try to squeeze your normal life in between accomplishing the many things on your wedding "to do" list.

As winter approached, I found myself breathing normally once again. The initial whirlwind of wedding planning had calmed. The framework of the wedding had taken shape nicely and the planning appeared to be on schedule. Feeling confident and in control, I put my wedding binder aside to focus on the holidays.

I have earned a well-deserved reputation for faithfully stressing out between Thanksgiving and Christmas, the result of my believing I can create Norman Rockwell's fantasy of the *picture perfect* family holiday. This year, however, it felt so good to have my mind off wedding planning that I really looked forward to the holiday season with upbeat cheer.

Taking a hiatus from wedding planning actually brought the focus back to Katie **and** Dan. And that brought about the question:

Where will Katie and Dan celebrate the holidays?

What newly engaged or newlywed couple does not face the dilemma of needing to be in two places at the same time during the holiday season?

The good news is that both Katie and Dan are blessed with very close families and wonderful holiday family traditions. The bad news is that Katie and Dan are blessed with very close families and wonderful holiday traditions, and until science perfects the process of cloning, someone will be disappointed. In the end, they exhausted themselves by trying to partake in each family's holiday celebrations, probably not enjoying a minute of it themselves. My heart ached as they arrived exhausted on Christmas night to join us for our extended family Christmas dinner. I can still see their red eyes and droopy heads as they tried to enjoy opening gifts from the family, and Santa, that evening.

Despite the rare opportunity of having both the Bride and Groom at home together, I never once asked them about the wedding. Even I was enjoying the break.

Not long into January, an unexpected winter storm gave me the nudge I needed to stay home, pack away the remaining Christmas decorations, and return treasured collectibles to their rightful space. Walking about the rooms, the corner of my eye kept catching a glimpse of my neglected wedding planning binder.

"Just one more day . . ." I thought to myself.

I called Mo the next morning to hear what progress she had made on her daughter's wedding. Misery loves company, and I could always rely on her to share stories of sleepless nights and endless phone calls. She then invited me to join her and several other new Mothers of the Bride who were getting together for a dinner meeting to share strategic wedding planning ideas.

Yahoo! I thought. Who doesn't enjoy a night out with the girls? And what a wonderful networking opportunity! I was motivated to get back to planning. No . . . I was EXCITED!

There are numerous publications available to a Bride and her Mother offering guidance on the Project Management aspect of wedding planning. It does not take long to comprehend the major steps required to plan a traditional wedding.

What I found through the school of hard knocks, however, was that PLANNING IS IN THE DETAILS, and the particulars are unique to each Bride and her family. What better way to get myself thinking about the fine points specific to Katie's wedding, than to hear others discussing the hurdles they were facing in planning theirs?

That evening I was energized by joining in the fun and discussions with the other rookie Mothers of the Bride. As we chatted up our daughters and their fiancés, the girls' personalities and their wedding styles, I jotted down ideas and tasks I needed to give more thought to later. I found a resource in the group that I had not found in any of my Wedding Planner Books.

At the end of the night, my list covered two napkins.

- Need vegetarian meal for brother Bill.
- Get Matt booked for a flight home. Best to fly into Providence or Hartford?
- Do we need food in the limo for the bridal party? Who will be responsible? What will we serve? No red wine!
- Hotel gift bags: Contents? Include weekend itinerary and list of recommended restaurants. Who will distribute? When?
- Book Tango into the kennel.
- Where is Matt getting his tuxedo? Chicago? Connecticut?
- Place cards for tables: Computer? Order from stationary store?
- Consider a cleaning lady for the month before the wedding.
- Schedule time for visiting with guests while in Newport.
- Talk to Katie about the need for a party bus to transport guests to and from reception and hotel.
- Print out a detailed schedule of events for the weekend of the wedding. Distribute to the wedding party.
- Plan family (only) dinner the night before the rehearsal dinner. Party of five.
- What is our involvement in Nicole's college graduation weekend? When does she start her new job in NJ? Final fitting for bridesmaid dress . . . when?

The women shared stories of weddings gone wrong . . . ministers having the wrong time and being MIA as the ceremony was about to begin, reception venues running late on a previously scheduled event that left the incoming wedding party and guests no place to park their cars or to mingle, crippling snow storms and forgotten essential lingerie.

I heard about the ensuing recovery logistics that saved the day.

One Month Ahead: Make seating arrangements and obtain place cards.

In the end it all works, but the build-up is mind blowing and with only weeks to go I found myself deep in the details when the phone rang late one weekday night. It was Katie.

"Hey! Dan and I are all set with our table seating arrangements. I've listed guests by table number and just emailed them to you. You can take that off my list!"

As I complained to Katie about my difficulty getting the number of entrée selections to balance out to the total number of guests, I located my glasses, walked over to my laptop and opened up the e-mail she had sent. Subject: Table Seating. The presentation was clear, grouping individuals by table number. I scanned the arrangement of the guests.

I knew we were not having a long head table like every wedding that took place in the '70s. The reception seating scheme would be 15 round tables with 8 to 10 guests per table. Fine. However, I had assumed the bridal party would be sitting together at the three round tables in the front of the reception room. BUT NO!

"Uh, Katie, you have Matt sitting at the Chicago table. Can we squeeze him into one of the bridal party tables without too much trouble?" I asked.

I scanned her email, but could not find any table listing, only bridesmaids or groomsmen and their guests. My eyes began to blur.

"We don't have the bridal party sitting together," Katie said firmly. "We're letting them sit at tables with their friends."

"You're kidding, right?" I blurted out, suddenly waking up. "You're spreading everyone around the room?"

Memories of our trip many months ago spent researching wedding venues came rushing back. *What the hell **was** I thinking?*

She, in fact, did not intend to seat her bridal party together at all.

"Mom, we want everyone to have a good time. What's the big deal?"

"Katie, your bridal party can suffer through dinner . . . all of 20 minutes . . . without their friends by their side."

"Fine, Dan and I will stay up all night and rework the seating. You'll have it first thing in the morning."

"Kate . . . (She will always be *Katie* to me, but *Kate* takes less time to say) . . . I have not asked for anything. I just feel that you put so much work into your bridal party that it would look nice having them all sit together. Besides, Kate, how are they going to know where to sit when they are introduced into the hall? Wouldn't it be easier to head them all in the same direction?"

(With a three-hour break between the ceremony and reception, and knowing the bridal party would be doing what most bridal parties do, I had a valid concern about this group finding their table if not clearly designated.)

Looking back on this exchange, I realized that we were both exhausted. Three weeks out and for the first time I did what I promised myself I would not do; I got upset over a detail that really didn't matter. I was being the Mother of the Bride that I promised myself I would not be. Only three weeks to go and we hit a wall. There was no way of saving the conversation before hanging up.

The following morning I had a scheduled walk with my next-door neighbor. Judy is a power walker and good friend and I think of her as medicine for both mind and body. I had not slept well that night, upset at myself for upsetting Katie. As I puffed up the hill, I confessed to Judy that I had argued with Katie about seating arrangements and was feeling bad about it. Mostly I was looking for a bit of understanding and support.

"Maureen," Judy said, "I have attended many weddings over the last few years, and to be honest, there were precious few where the bridal party actually sat together at the reception. Sorry."

I received the blow with mixed feelings. I wanted to hear that I wasn't the jerk I knew I was. That didn't happen. However, it was comforting to know that Katie was right, and I could go back to her, hat in hand, knowing that her choice for seating her bridal party was contemporary, socially acceptable and, now, fine with me.

I walked back through the door that morning much happier than when I had left for my walk. I quickly started a pot of coffee and fired up my laptop. Waiting for me was an e-mail from Katie. Subject: Table Seating – Final Revision. Katie and Dan had done a total rework of the seating for their friends and bridal party. The bridal party, including their dates, fit nicely at Tables #1, #2 and #3 located in front of the beautiful floor to ceiling Victorian mirror.

I knew I was forgiven and that she still loved me as I scrolled further down the e-mail.

Katie had me sitting at Table #15 . . . all by myself!

The MOB

I always knew the **Mob** was a frightening organization that you did not want to mess with, but I never realized just how frightening it could be until my mother joined.

Right around the time Dan proposed, several other classmates from my town also got engaged. In an attempt to share ideas and frustrations on wedding planning, all of the first-time mothers of the bride decided to band together and meet to discuss their ideas and plans for their upcoming weddings. My mother officially became a member of what I referred to as the Mother of the Bride (M.O.B.) club. In many ways, the M.O.B. club was great for both my mother and me. I have a feeling a lot of the venting and nagging I would have had to listen to was released onto the other members of the M.O.B., saving me a lot of grief and my mother a lot of agony. It was at these meetings that my mother could kick back and enjoy herself and feel like she wasn't the only one going through this sometimes horrible/sometimes rewarding thing called planning a wedding.

At first, not much else came out of the M.O.B. other than stress relief and the camaraderie it gave my mother. As most of the other women were planning local weddings, my mom was not able to take advantage of some of the information that was shared at these meetings. We had our venue in Newport, and we were well on our way to finding our vendors. It did help my mother to know, however, that she was on track with her planning. At each meeting, it became clear that we were either on schedule . . . or very far behind. Everything was going great until someone shared the revelation that a lot of money could be saved by buying in bulk. The M.O.B. quickly went into overdrive trying to become the Costco of wedding planning.

This is where things quickly went downhill. But, before I get to that, you need to know of an early childhood experience that scarred me for life. As I mentioned earlier, I am a huge animal lover. I was influenced by my mom at an early age when she started to bring stray animals into the house. We were, and probably still are, the only family that has had squirrels, guinea pigs, mice, parakeets, salamanders, cats and dogs as pets. One of my favorite pets growing up was my cat Tigger. He was a mellow cat who endured way too many hard hugs and tugs on the tail without ever biting or scratching me. The only time Tigger got fussy was when he had to get into his cat box and go to the vet. I'm sure everyone has seen these boxes with the holes in the sides that close on the top by folding into a nice little handle.

You can imagine how excited I was the day mom brought Tigger into my third grade classroom for show and tell. The morning that Tigger was to come into school started off as the best day. Waiting for my mom to walk into the classroom with Tigger in his cat box was making the clock move at a snail's pace. When 11:00 am finally rolled around and I saw my mom coming into the room I couldn't wait for everyone to meet Tigger.

I was surprised that I didn't notice it sooner, but as I opened the box the smell hit me like a ton of bricks. Tigger had shit himself on the ride over to school. My mom must have forgotten to tell him he wasn't going to the vet that day. Everyone in class quickly covered their nose with the sleeve of their shirt and my teacher rushed to open the windows and release the smell. My mom mumbled an apology to the teacher, shut the box, and took Tigger home. I was mortified and crushed all at the same time.

What does this have to do with the M.O.B. trying to compete with Costco? Well, among many items such as wine, ribbons and seating cards that the M.O.B. had found to order in bulk, they had also found a wonderful gift box to place in each guest's hotel room. Mom and I had an agreement that every M.O.B. order had to be approved before the orders were placed. So I was accustomed to occasional phone calls asking me to check my e-mail because another item had been sent to me for approval.

I was walking home from work one day when I got the phone call about the wonderful gift boxes that the M.O.B. had found during their last meeting. My mom was excited because the box was big enough to hold a bottle of wine and was going to be very cheap when ordered in bulk. Most importantly, it was less expensive than any of the paper bags we had been looking at in gift shops. I started to get excited about this new find and hurried home to check my e-mail. When I opened up the e-mail I thought I was going to die. Staring back at me was a miniature version of Tigger's box coated with pearly white paint to make it wedding appropriate, but not hiding the fact that it was, in fact, a miniature cat carrier.

When I got over the shock of what my mom thought would be a great gift carry-all for our wedding guests, I called her. After pointing out the resemblance of the gift box to the one Tigger was in the day of show and tell, we both roared at the memory. While it's true that nobody at the wedding would have put two and two together it was going to be way too hard for both my mother and me to hand over these boxes to the hotel to be placed in each guest's room without the image in our minds of Tigger covered in poop.

In the end, we put a bottle of wine and a wine opener tied with ribbon around the neck of the bottle in everyone's room along with a printed weekend itinerary and restaurant guide. This gave our guests the opportunity to have a little drink between the ceremony and reception without my mom and me cringing over what people would find when they opened Tigger's box.

The Wedding Day

A Marriage

I love walking into the TV room when Katie and Dan are home visiting and finding them cuddled on the sofa fast asleep . . . . Katie with her face nuzzled tight into Dan's shoulder and Dan with his face resting on Katie's hair.

I wonder what the future holds for the two of them. Will their marriage survive the trial and error required to get it right? Will their love and dedication outweigh their blunders and missteps? Will they have patience with each other along the way?

I am concerned that we may have painted too rosy a picture of marriage for the children; disappointments always kept private, problems worked out behind closed doors. I worry we may have set misleading expectations.

We were raised by a generation that held themselves and their children to a very high standard. We now know that to be happy in life, you must first be happy with who you are. How we discover that person will be different for every one of us. I pray that Katie and Dan accept and cherish their differences.

I find Katie to be focused and a touch of an over-achiever. I find Dan enthralled by Katie's enthusiasm. However, Dan also provides that balance of knowing when enough is enough . . . and when it is time to relax. A married couple's relationship is ever evolving. I am curious to see how Katie and Dan handle this transformation down the road.

I watch them struggle with launching new careers, nurturing this new committed relationship, planning a wedding and balancing what time remains between family and friends. I like what I see.

I watch the way Katie and Dan interact while making decisions. I am happy to see that on important issues like family and lifestyle they are clearly on the same page. I found humor watching them debate over the font style for their wedding invitations.

I observe the changing dynamics as this new person, my Son-in-Law Dan, is introduced into our family. Matt claiming Dan as the brother he never had; Katie and Nicole taking their relationship to the next level. Dan slid into the family all but unnoticed.

If I were to find a genie in a bottle, my first wish would be to go back in time, only for a time, when the children were young: Matt with his curly blond hair and bigger than life attitude, Katie with her engaging eyes and zippy wit, and Nicole in my arms with a personality yet to be discovered.

For my second wish, I would ask to be taken back to the dance floor in Newport where I was on cloud nine from the satisfaction of a job well done, the pride I held in my heart for my daughter and her new husband, and the thrill of dancing once again with family and friends.

My third wish is that my relationship with Katie continues to mature and grow as the excitement and challenges of the future unfold for her. I wish to find pleasure in Katie's independence and success, while always holding her close.

Man and Life

I had heard of the baby blues and post-partum depression, but I was shocked when I heard young women were experiencing the same sadness after their weddings. Apparently, after a year or two of non-stop wedding planning, women were feeling a sudden loss when the focus was no longer on them and there were no more plans to make. I thought they were crazy.

I couldn't wait to hunker down in my apartment with Dan and sit on the couch for an entire weekend and watch TV without moving! No more parties and showers where I had to find an outfit, no more panicking when I couldn't remember someone's name and, most importantly, no more wedding binder and checklist. It was going to be heaven. It turns out I was the crazy one.

After the wedding ended I felt a tinge of sadness as Dan and I headed off to the hotel. It had been quite a year of planning and spending time with family. And about as quickly as that sadness crept up on me it was gone. Had someone checked us into our hotel that night? Had we lost the room because we were checking in so late? Who had the keys and did I remember my passport for our honeymoon? All of a sudden I had a new list – the honeymoon list.

Dan and I had the best honeymoon. I'm sure everyone says that, but I think Dan and I really did. For two people who had never gone on vacation together or stayed in close quarters together for more than a weekend, it could have been a disaster, but everything was great. We had the same sleeping pattern, eating pattern and we both agreed that the cocktail hour should start no later than four o'clock. We had a full week of relaxation . . . and we haven't felt it since. Little did I realize that after we got back from the honeymoon we had one last round of social engagements to attend. We had to visit with each side of the family to reminisce about the wedding, show them the honeymoon and wedding pictures and discuss what we had planned for the next few months.

Who are the brides who have time for post-wedding blues? Are they available to help me clean the house, write my thank you cards, and shop for birthday and Christmas gifts? From holidays and birthdays to changing jobs and buying a new home we've been going non-stop.

Life goes on. The year of planning our wedding was a busy time. The year after our wedding has proven just as busy, but I must say has been the best year of my life, partially due to having Dan around and partially due to the lesson I learned during the year I spent planning the wedding. No one ever found me complaining about post wedding blues. I am now busy managing the contents of a three ring binder filled with my "honey-do" list.

Where Have All the Flowers Gone?

Our contract with the Astor Beechwood Mansion ended at 11:00 pm. This detail was taken very seriously. How seriously we did not realize until the night of the wedding.

> 10:30 pm: The open bar is closed.
> 10:40 pm: The band announces the last song.
> 10:45 pm: The lights come on.
> 10:50 pm: The tables are surrounded by wait staff.

The truth is: A wedding is the final chapter in the story of a bride and groom's engagement. All good stories come to an end.

During the course of the evening we are sure that mishaps took place, but everyone was having so much fun it didn't matter. The band took what we thought was a five minute break, but what turned out to be an out of control dancer who took the sax player out. The flowers were to go home with guests, but, as we hugged our guests goodbye, we heard Dad instructing the caterers to throw the bouquets out with the trash. People never stopped dancing long enough to have cake. It sat alone and lonely in a room with a full coffee bar and after dinner drinks.

By the end of the evening Katie's wedding gown was no longer the pristine dress she had put on that morning. And nobody cared. No one will see that dress again until it comes out of the museum quality preservation box the dry cleaners have placed it in for safekeeping.

As we hugged each other for the last time that evening there was no doubt in our minds that we would not have changed one thing.

So in the end what brought two generations together for a successful wedding? Certainly not an excitable, hands on, three ring binder carrying Mother of the Bride with too much time to think. Nor a laid back, information at her fingertips, laptop carrying Bride with too much else to think about. Rather, it was the humor and love between them that allowed these two unique personalities to find the perfect balance between the past and the present.

We wish you all the best!